Leila Cobo

DECODING "DEƒPACITO"

Born in Cali, Colombia, Leila Cobo is the vice president and Latin industry lead at *Billboard* and heads the Billboard Latin Music Conference. She has published two novels and three books about Latin music, including a top-selling biography of the late Jenni Rivera.

www.leilacobo.com

DECODING "DESPACITO"

AN ORAL HISTORY OF LATIN MUSIC

DECODING "DESPACITO"

AN ORAL HISTORY OF LATIN MUSIC

Leila Cobo

VINTAGE BOOKS

A DIVISION OF PENGUIN RANDOM HOUSE LLC

NEW YORK

A VINTAGE BOOKS ORIGINAL, MARCH 2021

Copyright © 2021 by Leila Cobo-Hanlon

All rights reserved. Published in the United States
by Vintage Books, a division of Penguin Random House LLC,
New York, and distributed in Canada by Penguin
Random House Canada Limited, Toronto.
Simultaneously published in Spanish in paperback as
La Fórmula "Despacito" by Vintage Español, a division of
Penguin Random House LLC, New York.

Vintage and colophon are registered trademarks of
Penguin Random House LLC.

Pages 305 constitutes an extension of this copyright page.

Library of Congress Cataloging-in-Publication Data
Names: Cobo, Leila, author.
Title: Decoding "Despacito" : an oral history of Latin music /
Leila Cobo.
Description: New York : Vintage Books, 2020.
Identifiers: LCCN 2020942283 (print)
LC record available at https://lccn.loc.gov/2020942283

Vintage Books Trade Paperback ISBN: 978-0-593-08133-4
eBook ISBN: 978-0-593-08134-1

Author photograph © Natalia Aguilera
Illustrations © Maria Ticce/Shutterstock
Book design by Nicholas Alguire

www.vintagebooks.com

Printed in the United States of America
10 9 8 7 6 5 4 3 2 1

The man that hath no music in himself,
Nor is not moved with concord of sweet sounds,
Is fit for treasons, stratagems and spoils;
The motions of his spirit are dull as night
And his affections dark as Erebus:
Let no such man be trusted. Mark the music.
—William Shakespeare, *The Merchant of Venice*,
act 5, scene 1

Contents

DECODING "DESPACITO"

AN ORAL HISTORY OF LATIN MUSIC

Prologue

Latin Music's Big Moment

The article in *Billboard* magazine read like so many pieces about Latin acts who achieve international renown. The artist had been discovered and pushed by the company's Latin American chief, but had become so successful that he was no longer going to merely release songs in Latin American countries. He would now be groomed for a major release for the mainstream market.

We could be speaking about Rosalía in 2019. Or Ricky Martin in 1999.

But this was Cuban bandleader Dámaso Pérez Prado, whose big band played mambo and other Latin rhythms. And the year was 1950.

The pianist and arranger, who, as the *Billboard* story said, "cuts in Mexico," had been RCA Victor's top Latin American seller for the past decade before the label decided to switch him from the international series to its pop label; meaning Pérez Prado was being taken from the Latin market and moved into the mainstream.

By then, he'd already made an impact with his "Que rico el

mambo," now considered a Latin standard, which he had re-released as "Mambo Jambo" for the American market.

But it was after that label switch in 1950 that his popularity exploded, in tandem with the globalization of mambo. By 1955, Pérez Prado's version of "Cherry Pink and Apple Blossom White," which was used as the theme for the Jane Russell film *Underwater!*, spent ten weeks at #1 on the *Billboard* pop charts, making it one of the biggest instrumental hits of all time.

The story of "Cherry Pink and Apple Blossom White" is one of great music built on quintessential Latin beats, of a fascinating bandleader and pianist, and of a groundbreaking moment not just for Latin music but for music and culture as a whole. The 1950s were about far more than Pérez Prado. The decade saw Nat King Cole sing in Spanish, the rise of Afro Cuban jazz, and the advent of the biggest triumph of Latin culture in Middle America: *I Love Lucy*, featuring Desi Arnaz, the real-life Cuban bandleader (and Lucille Ball's real-life husband) who played Lucy's endearing Cuban bandleader husband on TV.

It took more than seven decades to come full circle, to 2017, when "Despacito," another great track built on quintessential Latin beats, hit #1 on the Billboard Hot 100 and stayed there for sixteen straight weeks, a record at the time.

And "Despacito" highlighted a flood of Latin songs that came before and after, hits that found unprecedented global exposure, thanks to the rise of streaming services in an ever-shrinking world.

As of 2020, Latin music is the largest-growing genre of music in the world. Once considered the realm of romantic ballads and folk songs, it has blossomed to incorporate a dizzying array of subgenres, voices, nationalities, rhythms, syncopations, and styles big and small. It is sung in Spanish and in English and in both. It is inescapable.

But it's been a long road since the days of Pérez Prado.

In those seven decades, Latin music continued to seep into the fabric of popular culture, even as its popularity beyond the confines of Latin America and Spain ebbed and flowed, sometimes way below the surface of the mainstream, sometimes spectacularly above.

But even in the seemingly quiet years, when not a single conga or heart-wrenching ballad made it to non-Latin ears, Latin music—the term broadly applied to music sung predominantly in Spanish, regardless of origin—thrived. Supported by an ever-growing diaspora that refused to let go of the beats and sounds of their homelands, the music and its reach expanded relentlessly. The number of radio stations devoted to Spanish music grew, as did concerts and album sales. In the late 1980s, when I came to this country, Middle America might not have known the names Vicente Fernández, Luis Miguel, or Juan Luis Guerra, but all were selling out Madison Square Garden.

When I began working at *Billboard* in 2000 as the music brand's head of Latin music, the genre was experiencing a new renaissance: the so-called Latin Explosion led by Ricky Martin, Shakira, Marc Anthony, and Enrique Iglesias, among many others.

My timing couldn't have been better. I was Colombian, born and raised, but had come to the United States to study classical piano performance at Manhattan School of Music. After I graduated, I decided to pursue my other passion, media and journalism. I applied for a Fulbright scholarship and obtained a master's degree from the Annenberg School for Communication and Journalism at the University of Southern California. There had to be a way, I thought, to bring together music and journalism, music and media, my Latin background with my formal music training. It all meshed when I landed a job as the pop music critic for the *Miami Herald*. When the *Billboard* spot opened up in 2000, the time was ripe for Latin music to come into its own. The seeds had already been sown. In the mid-1990s, Gloria Estefan and the Miami Sound Machine awakened the world to the beat of the conga with music that was in English but had as its foundation aggressive Latin beats, a metaphor for a blending of cultures. It was, as Emilio Estefan famously once said, "rice and beans with hamburger." At the same time, the ultimate Latin symbol—the sexy crooner—had made its way into every living room in America, thanks to Julio Iglesias's and Willie Nelson's "To All the Girls I've Loved Before." Who knew Latin and country music could mesh?

But the Latin Explosion of the late 1990s was more like a tidal wave that enveloped the world, with Ricky Martin's "Livin' la vida loca" and Shakira's "Whenever, Wherever" serving as two of the flag bearers. They, too, became household names, eventually gracing the cover of *Time* magazine. The Latin Explosion waned over time, as pop music fads tend to do, but Latin music remained and thrived.

There were unexpected one-offs like "Macarena," a quintessential Spanish track from Sevilla, Spain, whose irresistible dance and beat made it a sporting-event favorite, and even the soundtrack of the 1996 Democratic National Convention.

At the same time, regional genres like the Dominican Republic's bachata and Colombia's vallenato built a fan base outside their geographical boundaries with the intoxicating fusion in the songs of artists like Juan Luis Guerra and Carlos Vives. Salsa, the New York–born mishmash of Cuban, Puerto Rican, and homegrown beats, found a socially conscious voice in the music of Willie Colón and Rubén Blades. Thanks to an influx of Mexican immigrants, variants of regional Mexican music boomed, from the mariachi strains of Vicente Fernández, to Los

Tigres del Norte's norteño corridos, with their tales of heroes and antiheroes.

And reggaetón, a distinctly Latin urban beat, came of age in Puerto Rico and quickly migrated North and South, with Daddy Yankee's "Gasolina" becoming a surprise global hit that introduced the world to a new, distinctively Latin rhythm.

In my time at *Billboard*, I have seen Latin music, and interest about it, reach unprecedented levels. Our charts have grown, our traffic has grown, our award show has grown, our annual Latin Music Conference has become a destination for artists from around the world, and our coverage has multiplied, in English and Spanish. Artists who used to be "ours" now belong to the world. Shakira, J Balvin, Ozuna, and Enrique Iglesias are household names.

The inexorable growth of Latin music led to a watershed moment at the 2019 Grammy Awards, which, for the first time in history, kicked off the show with Latin music, performed in English and Spanish by a group of artists that included Camila Cabello, Ricky Martin, and J Balvin. It signaled a huge paradigm shift: Latin music was finally viewed as a mainstream force with a built-in audience.

But to get to that point, there's been a history of hitmakers who paved the way with songs that have each, in their own style, had a part in determining Latin music's place in the overall tapestry of pop culture.

In *Decoding "Despacito"* I looked back at fifty rich years of Latin music and picked nineteen songs that defined movements, moments, and society, both musically and culturally speaking. Then, I set out to find the artists, the songwriters, the producers, the managers, the executives, the arrangers, and sometimes the wives and husbands who had brought these songs to life. Their voices are what you will hear in the pages of this book.

My selections were informed by twenty years of covering our Latin music scene and our Latin music business. Many of the interviews you'll read here literally span decades. Though most conversations were initiated expressly for this book, many have taken place throughout the years, in sit-downs with artists I've followed since they released their very first recording. Their growth has been my growth; their breakthroughs have also been mine.

Very few of our players were not available, for reasons ranging from health to travel. Even fewer have passed away. In both these cases, I sought out those who knew the stories behind the songs and the artists, and we dug deep to find existing interviews that were relevant. All told, I interviewed not only the artists but also more than fifty executives, writers, producers, and video directors, among others.

Is every song that marked a difference in here? No. There were, I admit, too many to include. It is my hope and my plan to feature them in a sequel, because our abundant range of music deserves it. But this is a starting point that spans many years and nationalities and genres. It represents an inspiring and comprehensive picture of the moments our music has defined in the past fifty years.

Beginning with José Feliciano's 1970 "Feliz Navidad" and ending with Rosalía's 2018 "Malamente," these are songs that moved the needle, not necessarily on the charts—although many did—but in terms of the perception of Latin music as a whole. They broke the rules and rewrote them; they changed the course of the business; they marked a before and a tangible after; they expanded the reach of Latin music and culture in ways that went beyond a mere moment in time.

In writing *Decoding "Despacito"* I wanted to bring to life the spellbinding process of music-making by telling stories that have seldom, if ever, been told. As a musician myself (albeit, one who rarely plays anymore), I tried to put myself in the shoes of these artists, and spoke to them as one musician to another, always coming from a place of great respect for the craft and the passion that underlies it. In my interviews, I found subjects who opened up without reservation. One of the great joys I take away from writing this book is the happiness I witnessed from artists who laughed out loud, recollecting stories they had long shelved away. Conversations that were supposed to take fifteen minutes often took hours. Such is the complexity and emotion that goes into making beautiful music.

From the salsa born and bred in the streets of New York City to Puerto Rican reggaetón and bilingual chart-toppers, here are the creators, the dreamers, and the optimists who believed in the culture and the music and, overwhelmingly, in the emotions that this music of ours can awaken, in any language.

This is how it really happened, as told by those who were there.

Leila Cobo

"Feliz Navidad"

José Feliciano
1970

PLAYERS

José Feliciano: Artist, composer

Rick Jarrard: Producer

Susan Feliciano: Wife, fan

If you could pinpoint the beginnings of what would later be termed "crossover," some of it would undoubtedly be found in the music of José Feliciano. In 1968, the Puerto Rican guitarist and singer captured the public imagination with his mind-bending cover of "Light My Fire," a vocal tour de force where the voice shares as much glory as Feliciano's guitar. One can find bolero references here, but, really, this is an homage to the Doors and Jim Morrison, performed by a Puerto Rican virtuoso whose music is as steeped in the blues as it is in Latin music. The track was produced by the man who would become Feliciano's longtime friend and producer, Rick Jarrard.

"Light My Fire" would peak at #3 on the Billboard Hot 100 that year, establishing Feliciano as a force in the business and paving the way for his 1968 Grammy as Best New Artist.

After that success, you might think that "Feliz Navidad" was part of a carefully planned strategic move. Nothing could be further from the truth.

Feliciano was working on an album of Christmas songs, with a couple of originals to be included among the covers. Jarrard suggested an original track and Feliciano came up with "Feliz Navidad" almost on a whim. The song became bilingual, he said, because he didn't want [to give pop radio an excuse] not to play it.

To understand how revolutionary, and prescient, this decision was, you only have to look at what the future of Latin music would hold, with bilingual songs populating the charts in record numbers five decades later.

As for "Feliz Navidad," its popularity grew slowly but surely through the years, finally attaining that rarest of standings: It's now a classic holiday song. In both Spanish and English.

Rick Jarrard

We've been friends for so many years. We're brothers. He calls me every day and every night and we end up having a Grand Marnier or something over the phone. A little *salud.*

My first record with José was the *Light My Fire* album, and that was a great, but exciting, challenge. I'm a great admirer of Latin music. Man, I love percussion. And that's one of the reasons I loved José and I always tried, even from the first album, I'd say, "Hey, José, let's toss a little Spanish in there."

And I loved it when he sings it because it was so emotional and so romantic. He is such an incredible guitarist and musician. I love rock, but I also love classical, and José had all those elements combined.

Susan Feliciano

When Rick first met José, he went to see him perform at the Golden Bear Club in Southern California. He heard some of the stuff he was doing onstage and drew inspiration for how the album was to be based on that, just building on the obvious. So he did a number of songs that were on the Feliciano album. As it turns out, "Light My Fire" was a hit the year before and Rick said, "José, you know we have a little time left, do you want to lay down 'Light My Fire'?"

And José said, "Oh, Rick, it was a hit a year before. I don't think so." But he ended up doing it almost in jest, and "Light My Fire" became "Light My Fire." Fast-forward three years. José and Rick have an extraordinary relationship. True brothers. I've seen him run to life going for José. With Rick it's real. It's not just words. They speak every day. They have for a long, long time.

José Feliciano

I never expected "Feliz Navidad" to be so iconic. I wrote it for a Christmas album that I did with Rick Jarrard, the same producer I had just done my English album with.

I was feeling kind of lonesome for my family in Puerto Rico, and Rick and I were doing the Christmas album, and Rick said to me, "You know, José, you should write a Christmas song." And I looked at him a little bit bewildered and said, "Rick, I don't know that I can write a Christmas song that's as good as the ones that are already out there. Like songs by Mel Tormé and his cohort." Rick said, "No, man, just write the song."

And I wrote the first lyric of the song: "Feliz Navidad, Feliz Navidad, prospero año y felicidad [Merry Christmas, merry Christmas, and a happy and prosperous New Year]."

Rick Jarrard

I love Christmas, José loves Christmas. We were doing the Christmas album, and we picked a bunch of traditional songs, some of which hadn't been done in a long time. I was at his house, and we were working together on the songs he had picked, and it's so funny because he had parrots at the time and they were screaming. I'll never forget that scene. It's locked in my mind. After we worked on "Silent Night" and the other songs, I said, "José, man, it would be great if you could write an original Christmas song." And this was such a funny scene, because we talked and talked and laughed and joked around. And he said, "How about this? 'Feliz Navidad, feliz Navidad.'" I said, "Man, I love that!" And he said, "Ricky, that is so simple, no one will ever like this song." I said, "José, we are recording that on our next session."

He is such a great musician. He felt the song was too simple, that it was not up to his normal level of expertise. He was totally serious about that. And I said, "José, I love it. We're putting it on the next session." And he said, "Okay."

That's one thing about José: We've always worked together and respected each other immensely. And if I want to try something, he'll try it. And if he wants to try something, I'll say, "Okay, let's do it." And he was open to that and we put that on the next session, and, lo and behold, we got "Feliz Navidad."

Susan Feliciano

They're working on a Christmas album, and it was supposed to be the greatest story ever told, and they were very careful in choosing the pieces and the instrumentals. It's beautifully done. And Rick goes to José, and says, "You know, José, we need a Christmas song." And José goes, "Oh, Rick, I don't think so. How can I compete with Irving Berlin?" And Rick says, "Come on, José." And fifteen minutes later they had "Feliz Navidad."

José Feliciano

And then I said to myself, "Well, let me make it bilingual, so the radio stations can't turn me off." So I did the lyric: "I wanna wish you a Merry Christmas, I wanna wish you a Merry Christmas, I wanna wish you a Merry Christmas from the bottom of my heart."

It just came to me; there's no rhyme or reason. The first lyric came to me, then I put the English lyric into it, not realizing that I had made it the only bilingual Christmas song ever in the world. I created a monster. Because this song has become the iconic Christmas song. Oh, most definitely. The only "Latin" Christmas record that you heard in English was "¿Dónde está Santa Claus? [Where Is Santa Claus?]" [a 1958 novelty hit performed by child star Augie Ríos, born in New York to Puerto Rican parents]. That was the Christmas song people listened to. Along came "Feliz Navidad" and it was something new.

I didn't know if we would get any kind of airplay on the song at all. So I prepared myself and made it so the radio stations wouldn't have any excuses. And now every Christmas they have to turn me on.

Rick Jarrard

No one else was recording in Spanish and English. They were not. José was really the first Latin artist in my estimation to have hits around the world, something that's been an overlooked fact, in my mind. When we recorded "Feliz Navidad," it felt like a hit single to me. But, of course, the odds were really against it because all the standard Christmas songs were out already, and it was a long shot. But it felt like something incredible to me and I always had that hope. Everything I produced for José, I always have that strong feeling that "Hey, this could be big." But it was a long shot.

José Feliciano

Rick and I went to the studio in California and we recorded the track. At the time I had my Brazilian drummer, Paulino, and he did the drums. I played the bass, the guitar, and the Puerto Rican cuatro [a small guitar, common in Puerto Rico], and I also played the guiro [a musical instrument made from a gourd, with a serrated surface scraped with a stick]. I did a duet with the bass and the cuatro. Listen to it and you'll see what I mean.

The arrangement was really between me and me. As I was doing the tracks, Rick was very encouraging. I wanted to put the cuatro in because it's a very Puerto Rican instrument. Venezuela has a different cuatro; it's kind of like a ukulele. Mexico has a different instrument called a vihuela, which they used with mariachis.

Rick Jarrard

I loved José playing cuatro, and I always suggest he do so if the song calls for it. He just plays it so well and the color of it is fantastic. Not very many songs will allow you to use it, but when it calls for it, it's great. We did not hire a cuatro player. Not when José Feliciano is around. He performs it himself and he plays incredibly. He can also play bass. You name it, José plays it.

We recorded at RCA Studios in Hollywood in the middle of summer, so it's a tough deal to get in the Christmas mood. José had just moved out here from New York.

I always cut José with a very basic track: very basic drums and maybe percussion and then we start overdubbing things with him. I do that so he can be free to really perform and not be locked in by a big orchestration. José is one of those artists who has to be free. So we did it that way and then we added percussion and the cuatro, and then built it up from there, adding the vocals and the harmony. We added the strings and the horns at a later date, and I just tried to change the various sections of the song using the horns or strings.

José recorded the guitar and vocals together. Sometimes we do it separately—the guitar first and the vocals later. But recording together is usually the best way to get a great performance from José because that's the way he does concerts—guitars and vocals. He's one of those guys who records the song from top to bottom versus recording line by line, like I've seen a lot of artists do. No, no, no. We do that song from top to bottom, and he performs the song, and that's how you get that great soulful feeling from José. It's one big, long performance, just as if he were in concert playing in front of thousands of people. We probably recorded extremely fast and probably in a single take. The harmonies took maybe another hour. He's such a fast

worker and player, and so proficient and so incredible that it
didn't take long. There are no questions with José, man. José,
let's put a harmony on that line. Okay. Bam. And again he's very
fast. He's one of the most accomplished, incredible musicians
I've ever worked with, and I've worked with some great ones.

José Feliciano

Nobody told me from the record company whether they liked
it or not. They just put it out and I have to say the song did
the rest. The album was called *Feliz Navidad* and the packaging
was an album cover with my name and a bow and holly berries
on it. It was a slow burn. The first year it had a lot of play. But
"Feliz Navidad" every year grew better and better and stronger
and stronger.

Susan Feliciano

I started José's fan club when I was fourteen. I'm Irish and Polish
and Eastern European, but I took Spanish in school. It was very
important to my education and José was a big part of that. By
listening to his music, I was told my pronunciation was quite
good.

After school I'd take the bus downtown and go to Hudson's
department store because they had the best collection of records.

The album was called *José Feliciano* [it was later reissued as
Feliz Navidad]. The original cover looks like a Christmas present with golden foil, a great big green-and-red bow and holly
leaves for the accent on the *é* in *José*. José wanted it to be a
present, because it was like a present for his followers, so RCA
maneuvered a Christmas packaging effect.

It was the only song on the album that I had never heard before and I saw it was something that José had written, which was of great interest to me. It was happy, upbeat, and bilingual, and easy enough for me to remember.

José Feliciano

The guitar I used to write it with is in the Smithsonian Institution. When I wrote "Feliz Navidad," I didn't give it much thought. I wrote it out of being a little bit depressed because I missed Puerto Rico and I missed my family and I missed having the lechón [suckling pig] with them. And that touch of nostalgia and happiness helped me to write the song.

This year I was in Japan, and they wanted me to do "Feliz Navidad" in the summer. And they wanted me to sing "Feliz Navidad" in China, where it's very, very popular, even though it wasn't the Christmas season and the Chinese don't even celebrate Christmas; they're Buddhist.

Susan Feliciano

We have three children who have grown up with it and it's something that they wear proudly. Johnny [Jonathan Feliciano is Feliciano's son as well as his drummer and tour manager] has a T-shirt that says, FELIZ NAVIDAD: IT'S NOT A SONG, IT'S AN ATTITUDE.

He's quite proud. They all are. I don't know if it's their favorite José song, but it's the one that has gotten the most attention and therefore it's the one to which they feel most connected. "Feliz Navidad" is like their baby brother. It's part of the family. I've never tried to put it into words before but, it is.

José Feliciano

Every Christmas "Feliz Navidad" seems to get stronger and always wipes out every other Christmas song on the market. And although I notice that now they play other versions of "Feliz Navidad," it may sound conceited on my part, but the original is still the best.

Rick Jarrard

Wherever he is in the world, it could be Poland, China, anywhere, if he starts singing that song, they'll sing with him. That phrase was not known in the English world until José did that song. And now, it's become standard. You see everyone walking around and saying, "Feliz Navidad." And if you say "Feliz Navidad" to them, they understand. It's become a part of their lives.

"Contrabando y traición"
Los Tigres del Norte
1974

PLAYERS

Ángel González: Composer

Arturo Pérez-Reverte: Novelist

Jorge Hernández: Lead singer, Los Tigres del Norte

The story was riveting. "They left San Isidro, [Mexico,] by way of Tijuana, the tires of their car were full of bad weed. They were Emilio Varela and Camelia the Texan."

So begins "Contrabando y traición (Contraband and treason)," a song penned by Mexican composer Ángel González.

Originally recorded by Los Angeles–based artist Joe Flores, the song became a hit among Mexican and Mexican American audiences with the 1974 version by Los Tigres del Norte, a then-fledgling norteño group made up of the Hernández brothers—Jorge, Hernán, and Raúl—and their cousin Oscar

Lara (the group is now made up of brothers Jorge, Hernán, Eduardo, and Luis Hernández, and Lara). "Contrabando y traición" was not a radio hit. There weren't enough radio stations playing it at the time to make it one. But its mark on popular culture is difficult to overstate.

Often dubbed "Camelia la Texana," the influence of this one single track has spanned generations of artistic and cultural manifestations, and continues to do so, unabated, today.

At its most basic level, "Contrabando y traición" served as the main launching pad for Los Tigres del Norte, who are widely regarded as the most influential, and most successful, norteño group of our times. Still playing after four decades, and with over thirty-five million albums sold, the group continues to embody everything that is both hip and traditional about the genre, not only making music, but, in the process, tackling just about any subject—from immigration reform, to drug trafficking, to politics—in their legendary corridos.

That tradition started with "Contrabando y traición." However, the song catapulted not just Los Tigres but an entire musical genre into the mainstream. It has since then found its way into literature, film, and television, and continues to thrive.

"Contrabando y traición" was first and foremost a corrido. Corridos are Mexican folk songs, with the accordion as their base instrument, that tell real stories of struggle, heroes, and antiheroes. They have been an integral part of Mexican culture since the Mexican Revolution in the early 1900s. Corridos evolved to become one of the most popular music genres in popular Mexican music, or "regional Mexican" music, as it's known in the United States.

The "narco" variation veers into the exploits of drug dealers, drug smugglers, and drug lords. In 1974, narcocorridos were not common, but they were certainly not unheard of, either. There are records of narcocorridos that go as far back as the 1930s, with songs like "El contrabandista," about a liquor smuggler turned drug smuggler, selling cocaine, morphine, and marijuana.

"Contrabando y traición" was also released at a time when drug trafficking was beginning to become a serious concern, very visibly affecting border relations.

Soon narcocorridos began flooding the underground and then the airwaves, and they continue to do so, having become part of the standard repertoire for most successful norteño groups. They veer from songs that pay blatant homage to famous cartel members to objective tales of deals gone good or bad, men shot dead, revenge, and incarceration.

But "Contrabando y traición" wasn't just a narcocorrido. It was also a love story, and its protagonist, the real badass, the one who ultimately pulls the trigger, was a woman, Camelia la Texana.

No corrido character has proven as memorable as the elusive Camelia, who inspired a spate of songs, including "Ya encontraron a Camelia (They found Camelia)" and "El hijo de Camelia (Camelia's son)," both recorded by Los Tigres del Norte.

The fact that Camelia's influence became the catalyst for the success of an entire subgenre of music is impressive enough. But it didn't stop there. In 2002, acclaimed Spanish novelist Arturo Pérez-Reverte published *La reina del sur* (*Queen of the South*), a novel inspired directly by "Contrabando y traición," which told the story of another female drug dealer, Teresa Mendoza. The story, the author of the novel claimed, was not real. But it could have been. It became a bestseller around the world and inspired Los Tigres to record both a corrido and an album, also titled *La reina del sur*.

And that wasn't all. Pérez-Reverte's book was turned into a soap opera, the most successful ever at the time for the Telemundo network. USA Network released its own *Queen of the South*. They are but two of many narco-inspired productions that continue to be among the most viewed programs on cable TV, network television, and streaming services, including *Narcos*, the successful Netflix series based on the illegal drug trade in Colombia. A companion series, *Narcos Mexico*, broadcast its first season in 2018, with an episode titled "Jefe de jefes (Boss of bosses)," not coincidentally the title of a Tigres del Norte narcocorrido.

Jorge Hernández

The song was produced by [the late] Art Walker. He was an Englishman we met in San José [California] and we called him Arturo Caminante, in Spanish. He had just arrived from Manchester, England, and we had arrived from Mexico. He didn't speak Spanish, and we didn't speak English. We communicated in sign language. I learned English with him and he learned Spanish with me.

Arturo was like a father to us. The people who brought us to the United States left and took our passports with them, and left us in San José with no money. We needed to work to make a living and we started to play in restaurants for money. Once a week, there was a Latin hour on the radio from a place called Pink Elephant (Pink Elephant Bakery, which still exists and is known for its Mexican pan dulce). We went there and asked if [the DJ] would give us a chance to perform on the show, so people could listen to us and hopefully hire us to play at parties and baptisms.

That's where Arturo heard us. One day he came to the show and he took us to the recording studio and we worked with him for fifteen years.

The song "Contrabando y traición" came out of Los Angeles, California. When I arrived to the United States in 1968, I was a minor. But Arturo had heard the song from a man who performed it live in a bar and he took us there. I was looking for something that would allow us to be known. By then we had recorded four albums, and nothing was happening. We needed a hit song that audiences would recognize.

So Arturo took us to hear this man. He said the song had something very important in it and that every time this man performed it in that Los Angeles club, people loved it. He took me there to meet this guy. His name was Ángel González, and he imitated Pedro Infante. He was a singer and a composer from Chihuahua, and he gave us the song. He died a few years ago.

Ángel González*

I arrived there [in the United States] with the idea of recording my songs—by then I had some thirty or forty songs done—because people had told me that there was plenty of local talent there, and that it was easy to record and to introduce new songs because there was not much competition with other composers. And I have a married sister there, so I went. And I had the good luck to enter with the right foot. That's one of the great things about the United States, that there an inventor who has invented something can get people to hear what he has to say, to listen to him and pay attention to him.

---

* Ángel González's quotes are taken from Elijah Wald, *Narcocorrido: A Journey into the Music of Drugs, Guns, and Guerrillas* (New York: Rayo, 2001). González died in 2005. This comes from chapter 1, "The Father of Camelia."

Jorge Hernández

My friends took me around back, and we saw him sing. He gave me the song, and that's the song that made us take off. But it was a very strange song. He sang it like a love song. About a flower, a very beautiful flower. He told me that's why he wrote it. That he loved camellias. It was a love song, but it was very commercial and I thought it would capture people's attention. When I saw the lyrics, we started to figure out how this person sang it, and how we would sing it.

Ángel González

My other songs are about social problems . . . problems in a marriage, the problems a son has with his parents. That's the sort of thing I like to write about. The only song of mine that doesn't have any message is "Contrabando y traición." . . . When I wrote that corrido, I was working on another project, on another song, and it wasn't coming. So I put that one aside, and then the rhymes began coming to me, and it just came and came and came.

Jorge Hernández

The song had that naughty element that we hadn't dared sing about back then. Back then, speaking about the things everyone openly talks about now was a little bit forbidden. Everything was a little more reserved.

We began our career singing corridos, but corridos about horses. There were also stories about certain personalities that we got asked to sing a lot. The story of Joaquín Murrieta, who stole from the rich and defended the poor back in the '40s and '50s. We'd also sung the story of a woman, called "Juanita la traicionera." We sang songs about horses, about towns, the stories of Pancho Villa and Emiliano Zapata. Things people requested and we learned by heart. But when we came to the border in the United States, that's when we started to learn the stories that happened here. We didn't know those stories. Here in California, we were taught the corridos of the border. We had never sung about contraband before. There was a song called "El contrabando del Paso [The El Paso contraband]," but it was about a man who was caught smuggling and sent to jail. We had never done a love story like that about Camelia, told from the perspectives of the man and the woman. That was also a novelty. That this was a story between the man and the woman. These stories tend to be all about men.

Ángel González

[The story is made up.] In Los Angeles I met a friend named Camelia, but she isn't from Texas. And there is an Emilio Varela in my family, but they don't even know each other. I am a feminist, 500 percent. A feminist is a man who knows what a woman is worth, who knows that woman is the greatest. Why is woman the greatest? Because woman is half the world, and what's more she's the mother of the other half. In my songs, I always have the woman come out ahead. "Contrabando y traición" was the first song like that. There was nothing like it.

Jorge Hernández

This was all new. There were other stories, but it was about alcohol prohibition. Al Capone. Or stories about men. Yes, there were older drug corridos, but not like this. We went to the recording studio and that's where we discovered our style of singing. We didn't sing solo. We sang everything as a duet. That's the way it was done back then. That song was in a key I couldn't really sing: too high or too low. I was kind of in the middle. And at the time, my voice was still very childlike, very thin. I thought the key didn't work and my voice was very, very tinny. When we went to the studio, we developed what Los Tigres is today. Art Walker said, "You can't sing it as a duet; you have to sing it alone." Hernán got so upset, he left the studio in a huff. To calm him down, we had to take a break for two, three hours.

We had to work on the style. On the pronunciation. The vocals in that song were recorded five times. Everything is doubled. Because my voice wasn't strong enough. It sounded childlike. Arturo would say: "Do it again, do it again, do it again." We changed our style and also a couple of the lyrics.

Back then, they didn't have the recording technology they have today, so I have no idea what miracles the recording engineer worked. But you had to record a single take. We put it out as a single: Side A was "Contrabando y traición" and Side B was "El porro Colombiano [The Colombian porro]." I always liked to record songs from other countries.

We finished, we took it with us, and we said, "Let's see what happens." We used to go with Arturo to the flea market on Sundays, and we'd sell music. We had a record player and we would play songs by different groups. We played the song, and people would be walking by and they would turn around and ask what it was. That's when we realized it could be a hit—when people heard it at the flea market.

Suddenly the song became something else. Fans started listening to it, each in their own way and each giving it their own meaning.

Ángel González

[About smuggling drugs in car tires:] There was no earlier example of someone doing that, but, if you use your head, where can the grass be most completely hidden? It must have occurred to someone to smuggle it in the tires.

The smugglers are like the mojados [literally "wetbacks," illegal migrants]; they know all the tricks and try out every possibility. . . . That song, I wrote it without thinking, I had no idea what would happen afterward. After my corrido, along came that whole pile of songs about drug traffickers, but I wrote it without any idea of that. It was a problem [that] I brought to light, but not something I knew much about. I hadn't seen any smugglers or anything. This traffic is something that was, is, and is going to continue being a problem on all the borders of the world. That's how it is, but I never never ever, thought that the song would make it big. Because my songs are something else, they are songs with a message, things from people's daily lives, and those songs aren't.

Jorge Hernández

It was a love song. When I began to sing it, when fans began to support it, I never thought of it as a drug song. I thought it was about a woman's very deep love, because she took his life away. It was about passion, but also about a very pure love because she was so jealous. We always said jealousy kills. Listeners latched onto the drug part because the drugs go inside the tires. It was

like, "Ah, we never thought drugs could be smuggled that way."
That was surprising back then. But also, to date, it's like an
anthem for all kinds of people in terms of love, in terms of
passion and betrayal, whether the man betrays the woman or
the woman betrays the man. Young people fall in love with the
song because it's a love song. She feels such a pure love for him,
and he didn't care. Kids today tell us that nothing has changed.

But it doesn't matter how much I say it's a love song, listeners
have it catalogued as something different. This song has been
transformed and every day it seems to acquire a different dimen-
sion. I don't know how to describe it anymore: as a song about
politics, a love song, or simply a reflection of the way men and
women behave with each other. We became good friends with
the composer. And we recorded many hits by him. His songs
were as if he were narrating a film or a documentary.

Arturo Pérez-Reverte told us he was at a bar in Mexico City
the first time he heard the song, and began to investigate its
origins. He came to us and spent some time in the state of
Culiacán, documenting the story of Camelia, and created the
character of Teresa la Mexicana.

Arturo Pérez-Reverte*

*Many years ago, I heard this corrido called "Camelia la Tejana
[Contrabando y traición]." I said, "What world is this that I don't
know, but seems fascinating." In the good and in the bad. In the*

---

* Arturo Pérez-Reverte's quotes are taken from the 2002 TV show *Al
100 x Sinaloa*. "Arturo Pérez-Reverte. Entrevista en México. 2002," YouTube
video, 58:31, "Zyra Dow," January 2, 2016, https://www.youtube
.com/watch?v=n4xRCDf4RUg&t=960s.

negative and in their codes of conduct. I started listening to narco-corridos, and, little by little, I got immersed in that world through music. One day, I felt the need to tell a Mexican story. And I came here [Culiacán, Sinaloa] to make sure it was the right setting for the story. And it was.

Jorge Hernández

When they called to ask if I could write a song about a book someone had written in Spain, I asked them to send the book to me. I read it, and said, "Of course." When I found out he had spent time in Culiacán, I paid more attention. I always thought "Contrabando y traición" would be interesting. When the song first came out, within two months, we were known in both Mexico and the United States. In the '70s, that kind of quick success was very hard. But with that song, within two, three months they were asking us to be in movies. They did a play about Camelia. It made me think it was going to last a long time. Every time we went out to sing it, the ovation was enormous. It felt difficult. Although I never thought it was going to be relevant for so long. We got film offers and a director hired us to do a movie called *La banda del carro rojo* [*The red car gang*]. Intellectuals began to seek us out. I met with writers and authors. It was weird because I had never had that experience. To date, they invite me to speak at conferences, in schools, at universities, to talk about the meaning of the song and the band.

"To All the Girls I've Loved Before"
Julio Iglesias & Willie Nelson
1984

PLAYERS

Albert Hammond: Songwriter, associate producer

Julio Iglesias: Singer

Willie Nelson: Singer

In 1984, the notion of a "crossover" was nonexistent. José Feliciano had pierced the surface with "Feliz Navidad" fourteen years before, but since then, there wasn't a Spanish-language singer who had deliberately tried to reach a mainstream American audience by recording in English.

And yet, Julio Iglesias was universally known. From Argentina to Canada, from Egypt to Russia, his was the voice and the face of Latin music. He sang in Spanish and in every other language: Italian, Portuguese, French, even Russian. Iglesias was, hands-down, the most important and the most recognizable name in Latin music at the time.

The man sold so many albums in Europe and Latin America that legendary CBS chief Walter Yetnikoff decided they should try to give it a go in English. "I spoke no English," recalls Iglesias today with a laugh. "Absolutely nothing. Well, I spoke a little rudimentary English but not enough to sing it." Although Iglesias recorded in many languages, he always readily admitted he couldn't speak them fluently. English posed an additional challenge. "It's not a question of whether I can sing in English," he said in 1984. "I can sit with a teacher until the accent is perfect. The problem in English is not the accent. The most important thing is the phrasing, the swing. Americans involve the vocals with the music in a completely different way than the Europeans do."

Iglesias had nothing to prove by singing in English, and, given his popularity and level of sales, little to gain. But he was intrigued by the challenge.

"We often think we're pioneers, and what's really pioneering is a country's culture," he says. "I was a Latin artist who wanted to do things in countries where I wasn't known. It was an adventure. And there were people who thought—I don't know if they believed it—but they thought I could maybe do something here. So I tried."

Richard Perry, whose résumé included albums by Harry Nilsson, Barbra Streisand, Carly Simon, and Diana Ross, came in as producer. But Iglesias remained tied to his roots with the help of longtime collaborators Ramón Arcusa of Dúo Dinámico (Dynamic Duo in English, a popular Spanish music duo from the 1960s) and Gibraltarian singer/songwriter Albert Hammond, already famous for "The Air That I Breathe," both of whom also took on production duties (Hammond is listed as associate producer).

The ensuing *1100 Bel Air Place*, named for Iglesias's home address in Los Angeles, wasn't simply an English-language album, but a testament to Iglesias's love of American pop. It included collaborations with the top names of the day: Diana Ross, the Beach Boys, Willie Nelson, and Stan Getz.

The album assembled a full symphony orchestra, plus the top songwriters, producers, arrangers, and session musicians of the day. The list is still jaw-dropping: keyboardists David Foster, James Newton Howard, and Michel Colombier, among others; guitarists Michael Landau and David Williams; recording engineer Humberto Gatica; producers Perry and Arcusa; and, naturally, the music of Albert Hammond.

The most successful track in the album was Hammond and Hal David's "To All the Girls I've Loved Before," which Iglesias sang alongside Willie Nelson. A 1986 video of Iglesias and Nelson, performing at Farm Aid, shows them side by side, almost incongruous in their differences: Nelson in shorts and T-shirt; Iglesias in slacks, a crisp white shirt, and a blue blazer with gold buttons. Who could have imagined that two such different men with two such different voices—one nasal and edgy, and the other airy and velvety—could blend with such seamless ease?

"To All the Girls I've Loved Before" struck a collective chord. It climbed to #5 on the Billboard Hot 100 chart, becoming Iglesias's highest-charting track ever on the Hot 100, and spent two weeks atop *Billboard*'s Country Singles chart. The Country Music Association named Nelson and Iglesias the Vocal Duo of the Year and the Academy of Country Music named the record Single of the Year. *1100 Bel Air Place* peaked at #5 on the Billboard 200, spent thirty-three weeks on the chart, and was certified four times platinum (selling four million copies) in the United States alone.

1100 Bel Air Place opened the door for Julio Iglesias to continue recording from the contemporary American songbook he so loved. But it opened a much wider door—one that allowed Spanish-language artists to view, for the very first time, the realm of possibilities available in English.

"Julio was the man who made the world fall in love with the Latin sound," Emilio Estefan told me many years ago. "He brought class to the Hispanic world. We've always sought out people who can make us feel pride, in a way, and Julio always made us feel proud. We were all trying to push, but he was one of the [key players]."

As Julio himself said, it wasn't just about singing in another language; it was the phrasing. Put another way, it was about taking a unique musical expression and applying it with boundless enthusiasm and the utmost care to another repertoire, another idiom, and, finally, another tongue.

Albert Hammond

I wrote the song for myself in 1973 with Hal David [from the songwriting duo of Hal David and Burt Bacharach]. I started working with Hal because I needed a new writing partner after working with Mike Hazlewood, who did everything with me from "The Air That I Breathe" to "Down by the River." I had to find someone to do an album with, and I looked and I thought Hal would be great. I got in touch with someone who knew him, and next thing I knew he called and said, "My name is Hal David, I'm staying at the Beverly Comstock. I'll see you tomorrow at 10:00 a.m."

Hal lived in New York at the time, so he came in and used to stay at the Beverly Comstock, which is now called the Beverly Plaza Hotel. We wrote there for fifteen days and we wrote fifteen songs. We wrote a song a day. The process was I would go home in the afternoon, I would come up with a tune, and I would go see him at ten in the morning, and he would lie on a couch and I would sing on a stool whatever came to mind and he would write, and we would have a coffee and chat about his life and my life and get to know each other. This was the first time we worked together and two of those songs—"99 Miles from LA" and "To All the Girls I've Loved Before"—became very big.

So I recorded the song, and I really thought it was going to be a huge hit for me, but it didn't quite do it. But I always believed in the song. When you believe in a song, it stays in you all the time. And every now and then I would get the president of CBS at the time, and he would say: "You know that song 'To All the Girls I've Loved Before'? I still think it's a hit." Then I would meet someone in Europe and they would say the same thing. And we went to Congress in Washington, DC, and Hal and I performed the song together. So the song was always haunting me and haunting me. And after mine wasn't a success, I even thought of getting together with Frank Sinatra and having him do it with Deana Martin [Dean Martin's daughter]. It stayed with me for like eleven years, and then Julio got to LA. We knew each other because I had written very large Spanish songs for him, like "Por un poco de tu amor [For a little of your love]."

Julio called me and said, "I'm making my first English album. Can you come over?" So I went and looked for songs for him. Things like "When I Fall in Love" by Nat King Cole. And then I thought, "Gosh, 'To All the Girls I've Loved Before' is the perfect song for this guy. He's a playboy. He's the guy every woman wants to have. I can't play it for him because he'll know there was a record that came before." So I went home and I rerecorded the song. And I picked him up in the car and said, "Julio, I wrote a brand-new song for you." And I played it for him. I had recorded it just with my guitar. And he said, "Oh, que bonita esta canción. Hay que grabarla esta noche [Oh, this song is so pretty. We have to record it tonight]."

Julio Iglesias

That song, even today, after so many years, every time I come into the United States, an immigration official will sing "To All the Girls I've Loved Before." It's a very endearing song. It has a beautiful story. The beautiful story is because of Willie Nelson. The rest is the contrast of two very different voices, the contrast between a Latin, occidental, European artist [and] a pure, strong country artist with a very special voice.

Richard Perry was the producer. Richard must have been forty years old. He was in his prime. He was one of three, four really important producers in the United States at the time, and I was doing the album with him. Albert Hammond was also with us, and, of course, Ramón Arcusa. And then we got the song. The most important factor here is that Richard Perry said, "We should do a duet with someone." And at the time, Walter Yetnikoff [then president/CEO CBS Records] had heard that Willie Nelson wanted to sing with me. The story is as follows: Willie was in London with his wife, and they heard my recording of "Begin the Beguine" playing on the radio at their hotel. Willie said, "Who is that? I'd like to do a duet with him." And that's where the whole thing started. He insisted on telling the label that he wanted to record a song, and this is the song they sent.

Willie Nelson*

I was in London listening to the radio when I heard a singer I liked. He had a distinctive lilt in his voice. After asking around,

---

* Willie Nelson's quotes are taken from chapter 25 of his memoir, *It's a Long Story: My Life* (New York: Little, Brown, 2015).

I found out his name was Julio Iglesias. Might be interesting to do a duet with him. Something different. Didn't matter to me if he was little known.

"Little known!" exclaimed [my manager] Mark. "This guy's one of the biggest-selling singers in the world. He's number one in Latin America. He's huge in Europe, huge in Asia."

"So much the better," I said. "See if he wants to sing with me."

He did. He picked out a song with English lyrics. It was something called "To All the Girls I've Loved Before." [. . .]

"You might want to cool it with the joints, though, Willie," said Mark. "Julio's a Spanish lawyer."

Julio Iglesias

I don't know who sent him the song, but the fact is, he said yes to the duet. We were recording the album in Los Angeles, and Richard Perry said to me, "Willie wants to record the song with you and he wants to do it in Austin, where he lives." We rented a plane from Johnny Cash, who had a Jetstream.

Albert Hammond

I got a callback that same night: "Get on a flight early in the morning. Willie is very excited about this." So, we rented a private jet and we went from Burbank to Austin, Texas, into Willie's studio and we recorded the song. The moment they met face-to-face was unbelievable. First of all, Willie had been playing golf and he came back with shorts on and a T-shirt, and he had a bandanna and the braid. And I said to Julio, "This is Willie." And Julio said, "That's Willie?" And when they started to talk, it was like magic. I showed Willie the song and he did the whole thing, and I brought it back and put [in] Julio's part.

Julio Iglesias

We got to Austin and Willie was there waiting for us. He was wearing shorts and his hair was very long. I turned around to Richard—we were still inside the car—and I said, "I don't think I can sing with him." He looked like a gardener. But then we said hi and he couldn't have been any nicer. After about half an hour we went to the studio. Willie smokes a lot of pot and I had never smoked in my life and everything smelled like pot. After ten minutes I couldn't sing a note. Or speak. I was toast.

Willie Nelson

A day before he arrived, I still hadn't heard the song.

Coach Darrell Royal, who was hanging around the studio, asked, "Don't you need to hear the song to see if you wanna sing it?"

"Hell," I said, "a guy who sells that many records worldwide is bound to have good taste."

Turned out Julio had great taste. He arrived in grand style. There were at least a dozen dudes in his entourage. When he showed up at the studio, he was wearing all white. Nice-looking guy. Perfectly mannered.

"Hope you don't mind the down-home atmosphere in here, Julio," I said, "but we believe in relaxing when recording."

"I thoroughly approve."

"Good." And with that I lit up a fat one.

No objections from Julio. He was focused on singing. He had a suggestion or two on how I might phrase the lyrics. The suggestions were good, and I took them to heart.

Me and Julio were simpatico.

Julio Iglesias

Inside the studio, they play the music and Willie begins to sing "To All the Girls I've Loved Before."

And then it's my turn, and I start to sing [sings with heavy Spanish accent]. Willie says, "This boy doesn't speak English." He stops the recording and says, "This boy doesn't know how to speak English." I apologized to him and I said, "I will sing this song in three weeks." The album was coming out in six, seven months. But the good thing is, we later had dinner at his house, and he was extremely nice and he asked, "What song do you know in English?"

And I told him, "Well, I sing 'As Time Goes By' a lot, because it's a song my father and my mother used to sing, and I know the words." So Willie gets his musicians together and the song was nominated for a Grammy [for Best Country Performance by a Duo or Group with Vocal, from Nelson's album *Without a Song*].

But that's just a little story. The main story is that when I sang with Willie I really didn't know how to speak English. At all. I did "As Time Goes By" because I sang it all the time at my parents' parties and I knew it by heart. But I spoke no English at all. I spoke a little bit of rudimentary English, but not enough to sing it. That's the real story.

Albert Hammond

Willie recorded in his shorts. I had to teach him the song so he would take it to another place. Willie had to learn the song until he really got it, and then he "put Willie into it." Just like Julio put Julio into it. That's the beauty of those artists. Something happened that said to me, "This is the guy who should do the duet with Julio." I could have chosen Frank Sinatra, but it would not have been the same. The perfect person was Willie Nelson. It was that issue of going against the grain. You two are not supposed to be happy together, but you are.

It was unbelievable. First of all, Walter Yetnikoff, who was the president of CBS at the time, said, "You're destroying my playboy with this cowboy." So I thought the best way was for Julio to do some duets with amazing people. I also brought in the Beach Boys to do "The Air That I Breathe." So you had Diana Ross with R&B, the Beach Boys, and Willie Nelson with country. I [spent a lot of time in Bel Air] with Julio during the nine months we recorded. That's why we called it *1100 Bel Air Place*.

Julio Iglesias

I was already recording other songs in English. By then I had recorded with the Beach Boys and I think with Diana Ross. But I had learned the songs phonetically. When we went to see Willie, the plan was to sing and record right there. That was impossible for me. I didn't speak the language well enough and I made many phonetic mistakes. Each word was difficult for me. To all. The girls. I've. Loved. Before.

What we did with the Beach Boys and Diana Ross was, they recorded their vocals, and then I spent a week or two on each song. So it was very different from just going there and singing with Willie right off the bat. He recorded it very quickly. Pum, pum, pum, pum. And I suffered, because I would say: "To all the geerls, geeerls." By the time I got to the word *before*, the music was way ahead of me. That's why we decided I would add my vocals later in the studio in California.

When we were mastering the track with Richard Perry, I remember as if it were today. I was standing to one side, and he turned around, looked at me, and said, "This is going to be #1 in the world."

Albert Hammond

Women react to this song because I think Julio attracts women. Whether it's a myth or not, the whole point is it works for him. When he sings "to all the girls who shared my life," it really is a song about all the girls one has loved, but sincerely loved. Not used. Some of them have obviously married someone else. I could count the girls I've loved on one hand, but I'm sure many, many men in the world have loved many women, and many women have loved many men. The song also works for women. Shirley Bassey sang "To All the Men I've Loved Before." It became a huge standard.

Julio Iglesias

The most beautiful part of all this is that I became good friends with Willie. He's a marvelously natural man. He is a natural. I never imagined I would sing with a country artist who was as pure, as special, as direct, as natural as Willie. Willie was the kind of guy who would pick up a guitar and go. He is a man of song, he smokes his joint, goes onstage and sings "On the

Road Again," and you go crazy because he doesn't even change
his outfit. He just goes out wearing whatever he has on. He's a
great guy.

Albert Hammond

I did all his [Julio's] English albums, except for one. I did this
first one with Richard and the others myself. "To All the Girls
I've Loved Before" is the biggest song Julio will ever have. People
all over the world will remember him for that song. That is
Julio's song, in every respect. Because of who Julio is. It's the
perfect song for him. . . . I waited eleven years to find the right
person to do it. Maybe the right person came at the right time.
If he hadn't called me, I wouldn't have even thought of the song.
Things happen because the universe decides. That energy out
there has a lot of influence over things.

Julio Iglesias

I hadn't fully realized things until now that time has passed;
up until now that time is so precious; up until now that life
is already delivering those blows where you stay alive by sheer
willpower, with the spirit God has given me to survive. It's now
that you realize that all those things you did, you did them for
the pure emotion. That's what's so beautiful about life when
you get success. That it's hugely exciting and you're still excited
when you're successful. It's not about riches. I'm not sorry about
anything. But had I known back then what all of this meant.
It's been almost fifty years since my story began and I wrote "El
amor [Love]" and "Canto a Galicia [Song for Galicia]." Then I
went to other languages like English, Chinese, French, Italian,

Portuguese, German. So many languages that I've sung in. And the excitement is what stays with me. I'm at a stage in my life where my thoughts are mainly about my legacy, about knowing how I explain to people the truth about everything. This was a very important song in my career. It was important for Willie. Willie still sings it all the time, and I do, too. It's still a vital song. My great crossover into the United States, into the Anglo market, is, without a doubt, "To All the Girls I've Loved Before." "Begin the Beguine" was a hit in Australia and England, but it didn't have that total crossover into the United States or even into other countries where they don't speak English and where I hadn't sung before, like China. It was my first big hit in Asia. That's why I have total gratitude—to Albert, to Richard, to Willie, to everybody who thought it was a good idea for me to sing with Willie Nelson. I didn't know who Willie Nelson was. But now I sure do.

"Conga"
Miami Sound Machine
1985

PLAYERS

Emilio Estefan: Bandleader, producer, artist

Enrique "Kiki" García: Drummer, songwriter

Gloria Estefan: Artist

Jeffrey Shane: Local promotion manager for Epic Records, now retired

Sergio Rozenblat: Then director of A&R and marketing for Discos CBS International, which later became Sony Discos

The 1980s were fertile years for Latin music. They saw the rise of legendary balladeers and songwriters like Julio Iglesias, José Luis Perales, José José, Juan Gabriel, and Rocío Dúrcal. These were artists who hailed mostly from Spain, Mexico, and Argentina, but whose romantic music struck a universal chord that enabled them to sell millions of copies throughout the Latin world, firmly establishing the viability of the industry as a whole. At the same time, salsa music from Cuba and Puerto Rico began to permeate other countries, like Colombia and Venezuela. But in the United States, Latin music and Latin culture in general were but a speck in the collective consciousness. Latins were almost completely absent from television. Save for the niche *¿Qué Pasa, USA?*, no Latin sitcom, or actor, had successfully occupied that space since *I Love Lucy*. Musically, virtually all Latin hits and hit-makers were imported, mostly from Mexico, Spain, and Argentina. With the exception of Julio Iglesias, the velvety-voiced crooner who was taking the world by storm singing ballads in every language, Latin personalities, and, perhaps most telling, Latin beats, were simply absent from the country's mainstream musical menu. Except for Miami. Although buffeted by drug wars, the city was a cauldron of cultural mix, fueled further by the Mariel boatlift of 1980. Here, Latin rhythms and culture mixed into the mainstream with careless abandon. Miami also benefited from its tropical climate and its location as the gateway to the United States from Latin America. Major labels set up shop there, beginning with Discos CBS (which would later become Sony Discos), the first Latin division of a multinational company.

The label was a commercial success, boasting a powerful Latin roster that included Brazilian giant Roberto Carlos, Spain's Julio Iglesias, and Venezuela's José Luis Rodríguez. But it had also signed local artists like Willie Chirino, Lissette, and a fledgling Miami-based fusion group that called itself the Miami Sound Machine. They were starkly different from anyone else.

Led by Emilio Estefan, the group—whose singer was Estefan's young wife, Gloria—saw itself as fully bicultural and bilingual. Much to the label's initial dismay, they wanted to record in English and Spanish, virtually unknown territory at a time when artists recorded in one language or the other. But the mix of aggressive Latin beats and English lyrics connected in the early '80s, a time when disco was waning, and the group found that its English-language single, "Dr. Beat," was a surprise hit in European clubs. It sowed the seed for "Conga," a song built on a Latin beat, but with a global sensibility. Its title was in Spanish, but it was globally recognized. The words were in English, even though the rhythm was quintessentially Latin.

The track was produced by Emilio Estefan, along with a production trio known as the "Jerks": Joe Galdo, Lawrence Dermer, and Rafael Vigil.

The group, the song, and the producers were all a mix of Latin and American, English and Spanish, or, as Emilio Estefan would so often say through the years, rice and beans with hamburger.

Initially viewed with skepticism, "Conga" gathered steam via a mix of unique sonic elements and passionate early adapters. Released in 1985, the track gained traction across radio stations and clubs all over the country and rose to #10 on the Billboard Hot 100 chart, becoming Gloria Estefan's first charting title (as part of Miami Sound Machine), her first Top 10 on the chart, and, with a total of twenty-seven weeks, her longest-charting title on the chart.

Gloria Estefan

It really started when "Dr. Beat," which was only one of two songs in English on our Spanish album *A toda máquina* [*On your feet*], went to #1 in Holland and to the Top 20 in the United Kingdom. We got shipped to Holland for promotion.

We were in Utrecht, which, funny enough, full circle, is where our musical opened in Holland in 2017.

We were taping a television show for a live audience at a club there. It was three in the morning, and we played "I Need a Man" and "Dr. Beat," which were huge hits in Holland. We didn't have a lot of material in English, and when we finished and they said, "We want more, we want more!" we had no more. Emilio had taken his accordion and he said, "Let's do our medley of congas," which we would do at the end of the night in all our gigs. It was literally a medley of old, old Cuban congas, most of which were in the public domain, that's how old they were.

I said, "But they don't speak Spanish!" And he said, "What difference does it make?"

So we do it and they go *crazy* for it in Holland. Afterward, I was standing in the alley waiting for our ride to take us back to the hotel and talking to our drummer, Kiki García. I said, "You know what? We need to write a song that talks about what this rhythm is. Talk about a conga, but write it in English. And we can do the same fusion that we did with 'Dr. Beat.' But 'Dr. Beat' is more like a 6/8 kind of feel. We should mix the 2/4 dance beat, maybe put a funk bass line or R&B and throw in the legitimate Cuban rhythms of a conga underneath it. I think it would work perfectly!"

Enrique "Kiki" García

It was customary for the band to play Cuban congas "from los carnavales [the carnivals]" as a way to get our audience to come together on the dance floor. We had played those songs for years and they had become a staple in our repertoire. It came in handy because as "Dr. Beat" becomes this megahit, the world gets to see a group with only one hit! In our shows, we had to incorporate covers and other fillers to beef up our live song list. We were in Utrecht in the Netherlands, playing in a club, and after we played our signature hit, "Dr. Beat," a number of times, the crowd was going crazy.

We ran out of songs to play. It so happened that we were elected to be the kings of the Calle Ocho Parade [the annual festival that takes place on Miami's Calle Ocho, or Eighth Street] that year and we had recorded the Cuban conga percussion track to use as a playback when we performed on the carnival floats. We would play the track and play live on top for reinforcement. So that night in Utrecht we let the conga percussion track fly and played the live congas on top. The club erupted into a giant conga line to our music, in Spanish, in the Netherlands. So funny how music unites the world. I made a joke about how it would be so strange that this song could make us famous.

Gloria Estefan

We flew out to England the next day to promote "Dr. Beat." We were so excited. We were on a high just being in Europe and having a #1 song in English. It was my first trip to Europe ever in my life. On our way to England, I was sitting next to Kiki on the plane. It was a commercial flight and we were traveling coach. I was sitting on his right and he started pounding out the rhythm of the song on the tray table and singing some parts of it. And we wrote the song right there.

Enrique "Kiki" García

The performance stayed on my mind all night. I could not get it out of my thoughts. The next day, as we got on the plane and

I sat down, this song comes flying out of my mind. I start tapping on the seat table in front of me and I'm singing, "Come on, shake your body, baby, do the conga." The rest was sketchy, but by the time we landed I had it all put together. I got up and sang my idea to Emilio and he loved it from the start. Emilio always loved my crazy song ideas.

As a writer, ideas are born in your mind and it's so hard to conceptualize how to get them on paper or even recorded. "Conga" was by far the easiest and most fun song I've ever written.

Gloria Estefan

The song has two chords. What Kiki sang on that tray table was literally some of the melody, which I tweaked and added things to, and the lyrics.

We came back to Miami and we were so excited about starting to perform this song, even before we went to the studio. It was the very first song that we wrote for the *Primitive Love* album. I remember being in the kitchen of my old house, literally taking cassette tape[s], and singing and scatting the horn lines in my head into the cassette. I gave them to my trumpet player, Teddy Mulet, and he wrote the arrangements for the horns. We rehearsed the song—it must have sounded a little different than what ended up being the single—and we started performing this before it was recorded. At the time, we were super popular across the pond and playing stadiums with fifty thousand in Latin America, but I still had gigs in Miami. Literally we would start playing it and the crowds would react as if they were hearing a hit song. They would rush to the dance floor. So we talked to the record company—they already had a huge hit with "Dr. Beat"—and we said, "We have it in our contract that we have the right to record an album in English, and we'd like to do that."

They said okay. Our budget was $25,000 for the album. [It was a budget] for a Latin American album. There was no way we were going to be able to produce the quality we needed to compete worldwide in English. So Emilio and I took all our savings at the time—it was like $65,000—and we combined it with what Sony gave us.

Emilio Estefan

I invested in the recording. I didn't have money left for the promotion. We were a young couple with little cash. But on the album, yes. We made miracles happen to have a great album. All the money went to the record. I always believe in quality. If life gives you a chance, give it all you have. It may not come back. I've always been a dreamer and I had to go through very difficult situations as a child. I turned the negative into a positive.

Gloria Estefan

We recorded the *Primitive Love* album at New River Studios. They gave us a lockout between gigs. For example, sometimes they had an odd number of days in between recording sessions and they cut us a break on the money, because it was super expensive. For "Conga," we wanted to do a remix like we had done with "Dr. Beat," and spoke with Pablo Flores in Puerto Rico, who did the remix to "Dr. Beat." When we met him, he was a DJ in a club called Bachelors and we'd been told that this guy did amazing things with our tracks. So we went to check him out while we were doing, I think, a Nissan commercial. Of course, we had no money. We told him we had these hours in the studio, and asked if he'd do it from scratch. He had never done this before, either; he had only done it at the time with fully made records. He was a neophyte. I said, "I guarantee that you'll make a killing on this, but we'll pay you on the back end."

When it came to "Conga," we did the twelve-inch, like we had done before with "Dr. Beat." We mixed the song, he did a remix of that, and then I said, "I love these parts of the remix so much, let's edit the remix back into the single."

For example, the song didn't start with the three horn chords and then the a capella vocals. That opening was a breakdown of the twelve-inch that he had created, and it became iconic. And, by the way, this was before automation. It would be like four or five of us, standing on the board muting things and creating the strips of tape to then put back together as a remix.

I approached the vocal part as if my voice were a percussion instrument. When I sang it, I really latched onto the consonants. That's why I never did that song in Spanish. Spanish is too soft. It doesn't have those sounds: "Come on, shake your body baby, do the conga."

I had to really grab the consonants and I sang it like I was a percussion instrument.

And then I had to do it in the three parts because I wanted to do an homage to the Andrews Sisters. That three-part harmony was very Andrews Sisters–like. We used to play the "Boogie Woogie Bugle Boy" with the band because I had a fascination with that. I wanted to throw back to a time when Latin music was just beginning in the US because that was the time of Desi Arnaz and all that. I thought it would be really cool for the vocals to be something completely unexpected, even beyond the funk-based line and the R&B in the song and the legit Cuban conga in it. And that scream at the beginning is James Brown.

We sampled James Brown. And we paid for the sample. Again, it was an homage.

Emilio Estefan

We called [drummer] Joe Galdo and he programmed the R&B beat with the conga section, and we got the best horn section. We were so excited. We thought, "Oh my God, this is so good!" Sometimes you love a song and you get enthusiastic about it and then you go to the record label. You don't know.

Gloria Estefan

"Conga" was produced by Emilio with the Jerks: Joe Galdo, Lawrence Dermer, and Rafael Vigil.

They were great musicians.

At the time we gave them this song, live drums weren't happening. "Conga" is programmed drums and live percussion. LinnDrums [a drum machine manufactured by Linn Electronics between 1982 and 1985] were the cutting-edge drums at the time. But we also created our own sounds in the studio and sampled them. For example, I took a giant book and dropped it on the floor of the studio, which created this tom [the tom drum is a cylindrical drum with no snares] sound that was very different. We didn't want to use sounds that other people had. Joe Galdo is a drummer, and he did something incredible, which is why I think "Conga" has stood the test of time: He would program the sound, but then he would go in and physically tweak it to give it a live sound.

It's a very unique combination of human and programmed drums.

We thought it was a smash! Before we even went into the studio, we saw the best focus group ever. And our audience in Miami was very diverse. People would flock to the dance floor as if they were hearing a song that was a hit. And that's very strange.

Sergio Rozenblat

I joined Discos CBS International in 1980. I was their first A&R director.

Gloria and Emilio were my project, and from that point on I worked every single one of their records. My first meeting with Emilio didn't go well. After we sat down to decide what we were going to do, he said he wanted to record half in English, and I told him we were ill equipped to do that. We just didn't have the contacts, the relationships, the penetration in the marketplace. I said, "Emilio, outside of Miami, no one knows the band."

He got really angry and got up and left the office.

And to his everlasting credit, he called me the next day and he said, "I thought about what you said, and you're right. But you can't talk to me that way." And he came in the next day, and eventually we became like brothers. We recorded in Spanish and then he brought "Dr. Beat." At that point I thought they were ready for an English album.

When I first heard "Conga," it wasn't like I thought it was going to turn the world upside down. It was a really, really catchy song. The challenge is how do I get it out there? How do I make sure that it has legs? It was the B side of a 45. It wasn't the A-side cut. [. . .]

The sound of the 45 wasn't as good as a twelve-inch. But the reaction is what convinced us that we had a hit. Everyone started playing it at the clubs, despite the fact that we had a 45. That was the first indicator of how big this was going to be.

Emilio Estefan

When we finished the song, we played it for the label in Miami first. Sergio Rozenblat was there, and they understood the Miami sound. They all said, "Wow, wow, wow!" They didn't say no. But they said convincing the people in New York would be hard. Up there, they didn't understand there was a very unique sound coming from Miami. So, we went to New York. We already had a #1 with "Dr. Beat" and they wanted to hear the new album. When we first played it, they freaked out. In a bad way. They said, "Radio will never play this in the United States. I don't see Y-100 playing this kind of music."

They wanted to take out the horns, the grooves, the tumbao. They said, "We love the band, but we're not going to put money behind something we don't believe in."

I said, "It could be crazy, but we're not taking anything out. I'm not changing anything. If we're going to be successful we need to be honest." Gloria was there at the meeting and she backed me up. We were really firm about it.

Gloria Estefan

It took a year for "Conga" to get to Top 10 in the United States. They kept telling us, "You're too Latin for the Americans and you're too American for the Latins. People aren't going to understand this song." And we're saying, "That's exactly why we're going to stand out. We don't want to sound like anything else on the radio. This is our sound. We know it's going to work. It just needs a chance."

And it took a guy, Jeffrey Shane, who was an independent radio promoter that Sony hired for us and who really believed in the band.

Jeffrey Shane

There was a person named Sergio Rozenblat who was the head of Discos CBS and their base was in Miami. I was in domestic and he was in international. I got a call from my bosses in New York at CBS Records, which is now Sony Music/Epic, and they asked me to go over and meet with Sergio and see if this project had any merit. I sat down with Sergio and Emilio, and they explained to me what they were trying to do. They'd had "Dr. Beat," but this was the first full-blown, complete release with full support of the domestic company. I hear the album, and I call my bosses, and I say, "This is a very interesting record." Everybody at the time was into Bruce Springsteen and "Born in the USA." This album had a lot of potential for dance, and I knew Miami would support it. I met with them a second time and we discussed the songs in the order we wanted to release them. Emilio agreed to release "Conga," "Bad Boys," and "Words Get in the Way." I told him, "If you release the songs in this way, I guarantee you a platinum album." They were all convinced we had a possibility. We already had some airplay with the local Y-100 station, and New York told me, "If you can get this record to play elsewhere, we will put more push behind it." So we came up with the formula of putting it on a twelve-inch single and sending it to all the dance clubs and pools in the country to see if we could get it high on the chart and then go to regular radio.

Sergio Rozenblat

I needed Shane to be the voice inside the company. He was a great promoter, extremely well connected. He was a cool guy, he had the gift of gab, cool guy, he was well dressed.

He was an integral part of my strategy, which was, How do I get to speak inside the company? How do I buy credibility? That's why Shane was so integral. We had to convince New York that this wasn't a little Miami band.

Jeffrey Shane

The record was initially out to the record pools, not radio. We had decided to show that this was a viable dance record, and it went to #1 in the club circuit. Then I got the record on almost every radio station in Florida, and on almost all those stations, it went to #1. So we got the #1 record in Florida, and now it became a priority for Epic Records domestic.

I called all the radio stations. I had really good relationships. I went and I said, "This has nothing to do with Epic Records. I am asking you for a favor to put the record on your station."

I was vested because they were from Miami and they were really the only band from there that I thought could make it. I was committed to them as people. It was exciting to get this egg from international and see if it could hatch. The excitement as a promotion person is to walk into a station and get them to play the record. In *On Your Feet* [the musical that tells the story of the Estefans], there's a character with dark glasses who says, "I got you St. Louis!" That was me.

Gloria Estefan

He literally called a personal friend of his in St. Louis and begged him to play the song once. And when he played the song, the phones went ballistic.

It was the first song that crossed four different charts in *Billboard*.

Emilio Estefan

We were doing a movie in Mexico, called *Club Med*. And while we were there, I got an urgent call from New York. And they say, "Emilio, you have to come back to the US. The record broke. Something like 143 stations are playing the song."

Jeffrey Shane took the song to Middle America.

And then everyone starts to play it because they'd look at the charts to see what was happening. We sent it to the record pools and they got a great reaction. And that's how it all started. I remember the first time we played on the Dick Clark show [*American Bandstand*]. You can see it in the people's reaction. It was the kind of song people immediately latched onto. It didn't matter where we were, the reaction was always spectacular.

Sergio Rozenblat

Then we did the "Conga" video and sent it to Europe, and they thought it was super campy. Little did they know that in Calle Ocho, those ladies, and the feathers, all that shit was real. We knew it would be campy. Like looking at a piece of art. It was a great time. To be in that place, the love and the innocence of the music. The love of the music drove us. And Gloria was ready.

Emilio Estefan

We were children of two cultures. I wanted to maintain that Latin side and at least leave a footprint of pride, of what we were. I think when things are done from a position of honesty and with a unique sound, those are the classics. Those songs that have been hits have always been totally different.

That's why I've always hoped that our career is an inspiration to so many new musicians and that people don't allow others to change their destiny.

"El gran varón"
Willie Colón
1989

PLAYERS

Marty Sheller: Arranger

Omar Alfanno: Songwriter

Willie Colón. Singer, producer, trombonist

Willie Colón's version of Omar Alfanno's tale of a gay Latino man who is shunned by his family and ultimately dies of AIDS was an unexpected success that has continued to endure. Because this was recorded at a time when the conversation about AIDS was just beginning and homophobia was a fact of life in Latin America, the notion that a macho salsa man would tackle such a topic was, in itself, revolutionary. More surprising still was the popularity of "El gran varón."

Included on Colón's 1989 album *Top Secret*, the track wasn't meant to be a first single, but DJs and fans alike embraced it and it rose to the top of playlists in Latin America and the United States, where it peaked at #13 on Billboard's Hot Latin Songs chart in June 1989. It was Colón's biggest hit on the charts to date. "El gran varón (The great male)" was an anomaly in every respect. It arrived at a time when Fania, the powerhouse indie label that took salsa music mainstream, was waning. Instead of the complex musical arrangements and socially minded lyrics that made Fania's catalog legendary, the tropical music market had shifted into the realm of "Erotic Salsa," a term coined to describe mid-tempo, danceable tracks with romantic, sometimes sexually explicit lyrics. Colón, a singer, trombonist, songwriter, and producer, and one of salsa's biggest names by virtue of the revolutionary albums he put out with Fania (including *Siembra* [*Sowing*], which he recorded with Rubén Blades) didn't fit into that equation. And yet, he insisted on including a socially minded track in every album. For *Top Secret*, that track was "El gran varón."

It would be naïve to think the song wouldn't be controversial. Many of its lyrics were ambivalently provocative. The line "No se puede corregir a la naturaleza; palo que nace dobaldo jamás su tronco endereza (You can't correct nature; a tree that's born bent will never straighten its trunk)" was deemed homophobic by some gay groups, even as some to the right accused Colón of condoning homosexuality by attributing it to genetics. Beyond that, "El gran varón" was well ahead of its time in its subject matter, candidly telling a story that was largely taboo. After all, how many macho Latin fathers were openly discussing their children's same-sex tendencies in 1989?

But "El gran varón" stood the test of time, the test of politics, and the test of political correctness. Colón eventually received a humanitarian award from designers Oscar de la Renta and Carolina Herrera, and the song's appeal continues to endure. In 2019, "El gran varón" and its title served as inspiration for a chapter in the Televisa series *Esta historia me suena* that tells the story of a transgender Mexican man who escapes his country to avoid bullying, but is ultimately deported and returns as a woman. *Simón, el gran varón* is also the name of a Mexican movie filmed in 2002 and inspired by the song.

As for the song itself, it was penned not by Colón but by Panamanian singer/songwriter Omar Alfanno, the man behind huge hits like Son By Four's "A puro dolor [Purest of pain]," and an artist considered today to be one of the great Latin American composers.

In 1989, though, Alfanno was a fledgling artist and songwriter, trying to jump-start a career as a salsa bandleader and singer at the same time as he was trying to place his songs.

"El gran varón," in Willie Colón's voice, would become his first massive hit.

Willie Colón

I was working in Mexico at a club called La Maraca and Omar Alfanno shows up and we're talking backstage. I had heard of him, but I didn't know him. We weren't friends. He just came up to me backstage and introduced himself and started talking. He was hustling. He had a bunch of songs. And he sang for me, a capella, a song about a guy who had AIDS and died. And I said, "Oh, that's interesting . . ."

Omar Alfanno

We were hired to open a show for Willie Colón, but at 5:00 p.m., when the band arrived, none of the members had brought their instruments. They thought the instruments would be at the venue. The promoter told me he was going to sue me if we didn't play. "Chucha madre," I said, which is a very Panamanian expression. And [promoter] Juan Toro heard me, and [he asked Willie if I could use his instruments and Willie said yes].

When I finished, before Willie went onstage, I went to thank Juan. I knocked on his dressing room door, they asked what I wanted, I explained who I was, and Juan waved me in. We chatted for a bit, and Juan told Willie—who was on the other side of the room—who I was. Willie nodded and I left. I was walking down the hall toward the parking lot when [I heard] a voice in my heart: "Go back and sing 'El gran varón' for him." Wow. I swear, it was the voice of God. I turned around, knocked on the door, and again they called Juan. I said, "Juan, my throat is really dry. Can you give me something to drink?" I can't tell you what they gave me, but I walked toward Willie, who was speaking with these journalists who were showing him a salsa magazine. I kind of sidled up to him until I was standing right next to him and he looked at me with this very New York attitude, like, "What?"

I said, "I have a song for you that I think you'll like."

"How does it go?" he asked.

I began: "En la sala de un hospital, a las nueve y cuarenta y tres, nació Simón . . . [In a hospital room, at 9:43, Simón was born . . .]."

And Willie opened his eyes real wide.

Who was Simón? When I studied at Saint Vincent de Paul school in Santiago de Veraguas in Panama, I had a friend I was very fond of. A normal boy, like anyone else. He had his girlfriends, played the guitar, hung out with all of us. He never ever gave any sign of being gay. This was around 1975, and where I lived, there was no room for homosexuality. It was like a sin. Like going before the firing squad, something terrible. Anyone who acted remotely gay was—the term *bullying* didn't exist then—but they were totally discriminated against. So I can imagine that Simón, which is not his real name, Simón withdrew. He had to have suffered very much. Plus, he came from a family of ranchers, of strong, rough people used to dealing with cattle. His dad was the kind of person that I'm told would rail against gay people when he had drinks at the bar. I think this boy, who had to repress his real self when he was little, had to have felt guilty, frustrated, all the effects of living in a society that psychologically castrated homosexuals.

Even us, his friends, we wouldn't have tolerated someone gay. We were all so repressed that if you were a guy, you had to play soccer or baseball. Forget volleyball. That was seen as a girls' sport. So many things I don't understand. When we graduated, everyone went their own way. I went to Mexico to study dentistry and he went to Argentina. He suffered there. They told me that when he'd speak to his father on the phone, his attitude was macho, superpower, all of that. But once he hung up, he would say things like, "Ay, I can't take this anymore." This was the late 1970s, and all those countries—Chile, Uruguay, Argentina—were in the middle of political turmoil and classes at the university were constantly canceled. He told his father he wanted to go somewhere else to study, and he chose a school in San Francisco.

Imagine. The place that affords the most liberties to the gay community. I imagine that after so many years of emotional captivity in terms of his sexual preference, he totally opened up. They told me they saw him walking the streets dressed in drag several times, although I didn't witness that. But it became part of the urban legend that was Simón. They also told me his father went to visit him unannounced, just like the song says. A woman opened the door, and it was Simón. What happened inside those doors I don't know. That's also part of the legend. But the dad was traumatized. That, everyone in our town knew. That strong man was felled by a boomerang. They tell me he got sick, he no longer went out because everyone would point at him as Simón's father, and Simón was gay.

When I was recording my first album in Miami, I met several of my high school friends and they told me the stories. When I asked about this boy, they said: "You didn't know? He's gay." I couldn't believe it. It was as if they had told me he was from another planet.

They're the ones who told me all these things. It stayed with me. I went back to Mexico, where I was living, and I wrote a first draft of "El gran varón" that I titled "Metamorfosis [Metamorphosis]."

I imagined him as this butterfly that starts to grow and leaves its cocoon and goes through this whole process. But I realized the lyrics were too vague, so I went to the root of the story my friends had told me and added detail. That's how "El gran varón" became "El gran varón" with that title.

Willie Colón

After I met Omar, I went on doing my album *Top Secret*. I finished and I thought there was something missing. I needed something that was kind of social, that could make some kind of social statement. I always include at least one track like that in my albums. That was missing from this album. And I remembered Omar's song. A year or two had gone by. I called him up and said, "What did you do with that song?" He said, "Nothing. Nobody's done anything with it." I told him I might be interested in recording it. And it's because I had a cousin who died at my grandma's house. I thought it was a cruel joke about a disease that gays used to get. Nobody knew what AIDS was at the time. But then we figured out that this AIDS thing was true, and I [eventually] called up Omar. The song was like a challenge for me. How do I sell this story? Notice I didn't say *record*. If I go to the studio planning to record a "hit record," I will probably wind up with crap. The next time I played in Puerto Rico, he was there, too, and we sat down and we talked about the song.

Omar Alfanno

I started working on my second album. At the time, erotic salsa was beginning as a movement and Eddie Santiago, one of the genre's most popular stars, went to play in Mexico. I was an RCA recording artist at the time and I was invited to his show. There I met Eddie, but I also met Angelo Torres, his band director.

I told him I was a songwriter and I composed many ballads that could be set to a salsa beat, and I wanted to record in Puerto Rico. He recommended a producer and the people at RCA agreed to pay me to go promote my album in Puerto Rico, but, at the same time, prepare to record my new album there. And while I was on the island, while I was at the [RCA] offices, an assistant, called Ilevia, tells me, "Willie Colón is outside waiting for you."

"Yeah, right," I said. The second time she told me, he was at the door.

"Hey, Simón," he said. "You got lost. Are you going to give me that song, or what?"

I couldn't believe it. Willie Colón was there, looking for me. He was one of the big singers who dominated radio and shows at the time. There was a king of trombone, and it was Willie Colón. It was every composer and every person's dream to stand face-to-face with Willie Colón. And that wasn't all. We went to my house to find a way to record "El gran varón"; the tape recorder I had didn't work. So, we got into this car, Willie Colón was driving, and I sat next to him with my guitar. I just stared at him until I said, "Pinch me, brother. I can't believe this." There were no cell phones, and I don't remember where we stopped to call a friend of mine who lived nearby and ask if he had a tape recorder. We went to the Regency Hotel, where Willie was staying, which, coincidentally, is the hotel were Hector Lavoe fell from the balcony [in 1988]. I sang the song for him in his room and Willie took the tape to New York with him to record the track.

Willie Colón

This time Omar came with his guitar and played the song. I thought certain aspects of the track were a little too hard, almost mocking. But I still liked the song and decided I would be able to reconcile those lines that I found harsh with the soneos [the improvisational verses that are integral to salsa music]. I added to the story with los soneos in between the choruses. That kind of softens it a little bit and adds a little bit more detail to the story. In New York, I sought out Marty Sheller, the arranger. He doesn't speak Spanish or anything. I explained to him what the song was about and the kinds of feelings we wanted to evoke. I recorded it in New York. With Marty I would do my homework and be ready for him and we would knock off a song in one day. Marty was old school. He was a jazz musician who played trumpet with Mongo Santamaría. He doesn't play piano per se. He arranges on it, but his instrument is the trumpet. There's a movie where Ann-Margret is on and she's dancing with Mongo Santamaría and Marty has the trumpet solo.

When I decide to go with an idea or concept, I will go all the way with it. I don't believe you can make a really good record quickly with a low budget. You need to invest many hours and find the right people to help execute the project. Arrangers, musicians, singers, engineers, and rehearsals to get everybody on the same page together. Only then can you create a track like "El gran varón."

Marty Sheller

I started my career as a trumpet player. I played in several Latin bands and eventually with Mongo Santamaría's band from 1962 to 1967. I played the trumpet solo in his hit "Watermelon Man." During that time, I got introduced to Willie Colón. He had done an album or two for Fania Records, and Jerry Masucci [the charismatic founder and owner of Fania Records] contacted me. Jerry was the owner, and said that he wants another album from Willie, but that Willie takes a long time to write out all the parts for his band, and would I be willing to have him dictate the parts to me? I could write them, and he would have the arrangements done much more quickly. The first song that we got together, he did exactly that. He had all the parts in his mind. He said, "Write this for the bass, write this for the piano, write this for the trombones," and we knocked off the first arrangement quickly. The second one, the same way. But the third one, we got into the middle of it, and he said, "I'm not sure what to do there." And I made a suggestion, and he liked it. That was the beginning of a relationship between us. Whenever he had me do arrangements for him, we would always discuss them in advance, and he would take my suggestions. And he was very smart; he would pick it up so that by the time we got to the next arrangement, I would know that he would use some of the ideas that I had suggested. That's how our relationship went through the years. Willie's a very prepared guy. In other words, by the time he gets to me to do an arrangement, he has already figured out basically what he wants. And because he's a good musician, he can explain it to me very well. It makes it very easy from an arranger's point of view to have someone with a definite focus. It's almost as if he were building a house. He can say, "Here's what the house is gonna look like."

In this particular song, we got together, and as usual he described what he wanted.

I don't speak Spanish. I understand a little bit, but not enough to recognize what the lyrics were saying. So he explained to me what it was about, and then he explained what he wanted musically. He said, "I want it to start off with a very soft, somber mood, and then it'll build up a little bit, and build up a little bit." I know that the voice is going to come in singing at the beginning, and this is what he's going to sing. When I start an arrangement that's vocal, I always think, "What is the best way to approach the entrance of the vocal? How can I best lead into that?" I wanted to write something that would be simple so that it would be easy to build upon. So I wrote that simple piano part. Then Willie comes in, and the bass comes in. And then, after the bass comes in, the cello comes in, so it's building slowly and slowly getting up to the part where it goes into the faster tempo.

Then I brought in the bass, and then I brought in a cello, and it built up and built up. Then he wanted it to go into the up-tempo section, and in the middle of it, he had a definite idea musically of what he wanted, like sort of a bomba type of rhythm. I remember him saying: "I don't want it to be like a typical Latin arrangement where when it gets into the coro [referring to the call-and-response section between the singer and chorus] and the soneo section—it's a long, long, long section. I don't want that. I want the coro and the soneo, and coro, and soneo, two times, and then a band part. After the band part we'll go back and do another coro, soneo, coro, soneo, and another band part."

And then he wanted it to go back to that original feeling, the slow, somber mood, and build up again to the end.

Willie Colón

It was not a hard song to sing. I liked that it has a lot of dynamics. It starts off as a ballad, then it goes into a guaracha kind of thing. It has a lot of parts to it. And then it stops in the middle and has this fermata. It's a pretty dramatic song. I recorded it with my regular band. It included [percussionists] Milton Cardona and José Mangual, and [pianist] Professor Joe. These guys who had been playing with me for years and years. We recorded on the thirty-fourth floor, at the old RCA studio at 1440 Broadway. Jerry had renamed it Good Vibrations. We would do the whole track top to bottom with the band. Usually I would do the whole band first, then the choruses, then the lead choruses. Since this room was so big, it lent itself to doing that. It had really great sound.

One of the things I really miss about "the good ole days" was spending the day with Marty. Marty has an extensive repertoire of jokes and he is very funny. We used to share jokes with each other. Unfortunately, as time passed we ran out of jokes and just kept telling the same ones over and over. Finally we decided to number them. Marty would say, "Number one," and we'd crack up. I'd say, "Number seven," and we'd laugh again. So Omar was watching and he joined in and yelled, "Number three!" Nobody laughed. So he asked me, "Why didn't anybody laugh?" And Marty said, "You don't know how to tell a joke!" I miss Marty. He was like a brother. We were a great team.

Marty Sheller

I was knocked out with the final version. Besides Willie's ability as a vocalist and as a producer, he knows how to get what he wants out of it. When I heard it, I realized that he's the one who also mixed it. *Mixed it* means getting the right balances of the instruments for the recording. He does a terrific job; he's a really good producer. As an arranger, when I write the music, I look at the manuscript paper with all the notes, and I know in my head what it's going to sound like. But a good producer makes it come alive, and that's one of the great things about working with Willie: Because of his great production values, he makes the music really jump off the page and come alive.

Not enough people give him credit for that. As far as the lyrics of the song, Willie would always sit down, and, line by line, explain what they meant. Once it got past that, I approached it from a strictly musical point of view. Just knowing what it was about in general, I approached it from a musical point of view.

Willie Colón

Marty was okay with the song. Marty knows what time it is. My wife did say, are you sure you're going to do the song?

It was good. It sounded good, it felt good, but it was still a very risqué topic to take up. Nobody was talking about AIDS or gays or anything like that in our macho culture.

Omar Alfanno

That song was like a "Bohemian Rhapsody" of its time. No one had spoken about this subject matter in this way. There were already songs like "Pedro Navaja," "Juanito Alimaña"—songs about the bad guys. This was different. It spoke about a forbidden subject, and I put it all in there. Especially the ending: "En la sala de un hospital, de una extraña enfermedad murió Simón [In a hospital bed, of a strange disease, Simón died]." I wrote "strange disease" because it was a strange disease. At the time, people didn't really know what was happening with AIDS. Gay people were dying. Magic Johnson was diagnosed and he left the NBA. Boxers started to take precautions. It was a mess. And because that song spoke about homosexuality related to a "strange disease" that kills Simón, it raised awareness. People started to scrutinize the lyrics. If you go line by line, it's a cruel description. It's important that people know that when I wrote the song, I didn't know that Simón had died, alone, of AIDS. I needed to end the story, and I ended it the way I thought it should end. It was only later that they told me in Panama that he had indeed died. That had a huge impact on me.

Willie Colón

I didn't have a label at the time. I couldn't sell the freakin' album. I flew all the way to freakin' Los Angeles to meet with Luis Pisterman [then managing director of Warner Music International]. I played the record for him and he barely paid attention to it, and then he says he's not interested. Before I left, I told him, "This is going to be a #1 hit."

I ended up going back to Jerry Masucci and licensing the album to Fania. Masucci trusted me so much. I would tell him, "Jerry, I have this idea: I want do an album with a Puerto Rican cuatro." He wouldn't even let me finish. "Here's the money. Bring me the record."

Omar Alfanno

When Willie went to Mexico to promote the album, I had a lot of friends in radio, because I had been promoting my own music as a salsero [salsa artist]. He went to radio station Tropi Q in Mexico, to a late-night salsa show. Willie said he was promoting his new album and the first single was called "Primera noche de amor [First night of love]." They said, "Don't you have a song called 'El gran varón'?" And Willie said, "Yes, but that's not the single."

They said, "Let's let people decide." They first played "Primera noche de amor" and then "El gran varón." And people started calling to ask for "El gran varón."

Willie Colón

Automatically, organically, all the DJs started picking that song without us promoting it. And it came to a moment where it was #1 in like ten countries in Latin America. It was incredible. It snowballed. I think I performed it for the first time in New York, and when we played it live, people really listened to the song. After it became a big hit, it was a very visceral reaction. Then I started getting pushback from [gay and religious communities. The gay community] said, "No somos palos doblados. ¿Qué te pasa? [We're not bent trees. What's wrong with you?]" Some religious groups said, "Who are you—the spokesperson for the gay community?" Sometimes gay people in the audience would ask for it and they would be crying. They really identified. They got the message.

After all the protests and after the dust settled, I guess everybody decided it was for the best. I can't count the times people have come up to me and told me that their loved one or their son died of AIDS.

Marty Sheller

At the time, honestly, I didn't realize how groundbreaking it would be. I just knew that I really was pleased with my arrangement. I was really pleased with Willie's production and how great he sounded. But I looked at it as just another good job that we had done together, not realizing that it would have the impact that it had. Of course I realized it became a hit and that it had done very well. But a number of years ago, I went to see Willie in concert, I think in Philadelphia. When he came out, naturally, the audience gave him a standing ovation, and he started playing a lot of songs that they were familiar with. But when it got to "El gran varon," I couldn't believe it. The piano started that soft introduction, and the place went wild; they recognized that that was the beginning of that song. It really struck me, that even though I knew it had been a hit, I didn't realize how important it was, how people reacted to it so well.

Omar Alfanno

There was a kind of rebirth for Willie Colón. And, for me, that's when I was able to tell the world I had written "El gran varón," that I was the composer. That song was very important. It's had so many versions. It became a legend. I perform as a singer/songwriter, and I always have to perform that song. I can unequivocally say that song marked a before and an after for me and for Willie. It's a song that has become an anthem for the gay community. Having written that song, with no pretenses, with not even the hope of getting it recorded, has been one of the biggest blessings in my life. It put me in a place that, thank God, I have been able to maximize, and I have never stopped composing. The one thing I'll never give out is the real name of el gran varón. In my town, some people have their suspicions. But when they ask if I wrote the song for X or Y, I just smile. Only my wife, Carmen, knows.

Willie Colón

"El gran varón" was a hit for me in every way: radio, sales, live. The more people talked about it, the more it blew up. And three or four years later, Oscar de la Renta and Carolina Herrera gave me a humanitarian award in Washington, DC, for recording the song. To this day, it's one of my biggest songs. I'm fortunate. I kind of stumbled into a lot of great moments. I just did what was in front of me. There was no master plan.

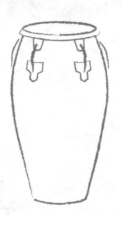

"Burbujas de amor"
Juan Luis Guerra & 4.40
1990

PLAYERS

Amarilys Germán: Manager

Juan Luis Guerra: Songwriter, artist

Roger Zayas: Singer, founding member of 4.40

At the turn of the 1990s, Latin music began to look within in search of its own identity. For years, orchestrated pop had been the musical lingua franca that unified the Latin universe—Latin America, Spain, and the US Latin population—with big-voiced balladeers like José José, Juan Gabriel, Ana Gabriel, Raphael, and José Luis Rodríguez dominating charts and souls with songs of love and hurt.

But in the late 1980s and the 1990s, a new generation of musicians raised on American and British rock veered into radically different sounds. They included Argentine rockers like

Soda Stereo and Los Fabulosos Cadillacs, Mexico's alt experimenters Café Tacuba, pop/rockers Maná, and rebel girl Gloria Trevi.

All these artists stayed close to their roots in both language and message, even as their music freely borrowed from English-language rock and pop.

At the same time, another musical movement was brewing—one led by artists who had also been raised on rock 'n' roll, but were meshing those sounds with the homegrown folk music of their countries.

In Colombia, Carlos Vives would turn to the accordion-based vallenato and the rhythmic cumbia of his country's Caribbean coast. But before that a guitarist and composer named Juan Luis Guerra left the Dominican Republic for Berklee College of Music in Boston to hone his musical skills in the realm of jazz and orchestration. Far from his tropical island, he had a revelation: His best musical output came when he incorporated his country's most indigenous and distinctive rhythms into his music. Those rhythms included bachata, the music of Dominican peasants and lower classes, mostly marginalized and shunned not only by the upper classes but also by most mainstream media inside his own country. Known as "música de amargue," or music of bitterness, its songs were about love and loss and treason and treachery, set to simple, plucked guitar lines, played in dives and bars and brothels and danced pelvis against pelvis.

Eventually, local artists like Luis Díaz and Victor Victor began expanding bachata's reach.

But it was Guerra, armed with his Berklee knowledge, his guitar chops, his Dominican roots, and his love for the Beatles, who made bachata truly international, elevating the level of lyricism, arranging, orchestration, and execution in his 1991 album, *Bachata rosa* (Pink bachata).

Prior to that, Guerra and his band, 4.40, had already notched an international hit with his 1989 set, *Ojalá que llueva café* (I hope it rains coffee), a progressive take on merengue—another Dominican rhythm—that captured the collective imagination of Latin listeners around the world.

Bachata rosa was his first foray into bachata, inspired by the music his uncle played on the radio when he drove him to school as a child. In *Bachata rosa*, Guerra took that "music of bitterness" and made it achingly lovely. From lush vocal harmonies; to melodies inspired by the Beatles; to impossibly beautiful, loving lyrics, *Bachata rosa* turned the concept of bachata on its head. Inspired by the poetry of Pablo Neruda, this was no longer rough and bitter and raw; it was sensual and poetic and arranged with an elevated sense of musicianship.

The linchpin was the first single, "Burbujas de amor [Bubbles of love]," the first of a string of hits derived from *Bachata rosa*. With guitar lines directly influenced by George Harrison and lyrics influenced by Neruda, it was, to put it starkly, mind-blowing. In the space of a year, countries that had never heard the word *bachata*, much less danced to it, were rhythmically swaying their hips to a sultrier tropical beat that was radically different from salsa, or anything else.

More importantly, Guerra's success indicated that even the "rootsiest" of genres could find international appeal.

Guerra and *Bachata rosa* spawned a bachata revolution that continues to date in the music of artists like Aventura and Romeo Santos. The ultimate reward? In 2019, UNESCO made bachata part of its Representative List of the Intangible Cultural Heritage of Humanity.

Juan Luis Guerra

I was working on the album *Bachata rosa*. My wife and I had just moved to our apartment in Ensanche Naco [a neighborhood in Santo Domingo]. It was a time in our lives when we were in the apartment, buying things, starting our lives as a married couple. We weren't just married, but we were in that process of adapting and living that life of togetherness. Truth is, it was an extremely creative period. Imagine bringing together all those songs in a single album. Aside from "Bachata rosa" [which gives the album its name], we had "La bilirrubina [The bilirubin]," "Como abeja al panal [Like a bee to the comb]"—a series of songs that would eventually become classics. And "Burbujas de amor" was one of them. The album marked the first time I decided to compose bachata in my albums. I hadn't done it before. I had that bachata foundation because my uncle would drive me to school when I was a teenager and he would always play a bachata show that was on the radio in the mornings. I liked many bachatas. I liked the guitar solos. I was intrigued by the vocal inflections; they had a very specific singsong quality about them. I wasn't listening analytically. I simply learned the genre without thinking about it. Had it been up to me, I probably would have listened to the Beatles in the car. But I had that foundation saved inside my heart, and with *Bachata rosa*, I decided to take it out and work on it.

Roger Zayas

Bachata, as such, obviously existed. It was like the American blues. It was a música de amargue, as we call it. Songs about the lower classes and people from the countryside who poured their heart out in those lyrics. That sort of thing. But it wasn't well-regarded music among the middle and upper-middle classes. It was seen as common music that they really didn't listen to or were interested in. They saw the music, and the way it was danced, as vulgar. But there were always prominent bachata singers. People like Luis Díaz, who started to write a very different kind of bachata that was then performed by more popular or mainstream singers. There were artists like Victor Victor, who also made a more "decent"—if we can call it that—kind of bachata. Describing it like that sounds derogatory, but when I use the word *decency*, I'm referring to the musical and lyrical treatment bachata got.

Juan Luis Guerra

Bachata is a kind of bolero—a Caribbean bolero that's very specific to our country, the Dominican Republic. I started to work this kind of bachata that was a little bit more sophisticated because the chords were, let's call them rock, very influenced by the rock tradition of the Beatles and by jazz. And, above all, I wanted to give the lyrics a different context. Although bachatas about love have always existed, the lyrics of my bachatas are extremely romantic and not as much about spite, as is the case with traditional bachatas.

I listened to merengue before I listened to bachata, but then I went to Berklee to study and my big influences were jazz musicians: Pat Metheny and big band music by the likes of Count Basie and Duke Ellington. All that, along with rock, fused together so I could create this style of bachata that many call "bachata rosa."

Bachata rosa is my brand of bachata with a different touch, marked by rock, jazz, and romantic lyrics.

Roger Zayas

At the time, Juan Luis investigated a lot and he went deep in order to extract the essence. The same thing happened with *Ojalá que llueva café* (his 1989 merengue album), which was the result of investigative fieldwork. Looking to always make a difference and not repeat the formula of the previous album, he decided to investigate bachata and make his own style of music that broke ranks with everything that had been done before.

We were always rockers since we were teens, Juan Luis and I. And we were in the studio together a lot even before we became 4.40 and all of that. And to suddenly see ourselves exploiting our own music is incredibly valuable. To be able to add all those different elements that he added to all those songs that were alien to us, so to speak, because they weren't in our nature as musicians. But Juan Luis was able to fuse his own guitar style. The overall sound of the song is what made the difference. If you listen to old bachatas, the sound is primitive, rustic, heartbreaking. The blues of the '50s is similar. Even if you listen to Romeo Santos's bachata, for example, the guitars have a more strident sound, the sound of bachata from the streets, from the fields. Because Juan Luis is a guitarist, his guitars were always influenced by one of his heroes or by his own sound, which is, let's say, more developed, more elegant, not as strident. It's a sound designed to make it different and give it that class he wanted to take the music to.

Juan Luis Guerra

Everything I do is through my guitar. I take the guitar, I start to sing, and many times I'm inspired by something I've seen or read. In the case of "Burbujas," I was reading *Rayuela*, the novel by Julio Cortázar. That's what partly inspired the lyrics. There's a character in the novel who literally presses his nose against a fishbowl to see the fish.

[In *Rayuela*, La Maga says, "I think fish no longer want to leave the fishbowl. They rarely press their noses against the glass."] It was one of those songs that just come out fully formed. There are songs that require a lot of work, and some don't. They're just born. This was one of them. [The lyrics to "Burbujas de amor" that Guerra alludes to here are as follows: "I'd like to be a fish, to press my nose against your fishbowl, make bubbles of love everywhere and spend the night, soaked in you."]

Roger Zayas

He was inspired by the Cortázar story that brings up that image of a fish touching the fishbowl with his little mouth, because fish don't have noses. I've always said Juan Luis has the gift of melody, and it's also very easy for him to develop poetic and literary ideas. At the time, he was really, really into Cortázar, García Lorca, and Neruda. And that's why he dedicates the song "Bachata rosa" to Pablo Neruda. There's a line that he takes from a Neruda poem. [The poem is "El libro de las preguntas [The book of questions]," which has the line "Tell me, is the rose naked, or is that only a dress?" The opening words of "Bachata rosa" are "I'll give you a rose. I found it on the road. I don't know if it's naked, or if it only has one dress."]

Juan Luis Guerra

My writing process always starts with the melody, not the lyrics. Maybe there will be a chorus with a few words, but not the entire thing. After I finish the entire song—the melody—I harmonize more and I start the arrangement. I used to have to write all those arrangements on sheet music, but now, with home studios, of course, the process is different.

"Burbujas" starts with a guitar solo, which is the way many of the bachatas I listened to with my uncle began. I also wanted to add a solo trumpet with a mute, which is also common in jazz. Miles Davis used that kind of mute.

And there's a very notable influence from the Beatles in the choruses. I learned every song by the Beatles, and I knew how to harmonize them. That's what I did. That influence of the Beatles in the chorus, and the guitar style, of course, is very clear in my bachatas. It was like bringing the world of rock into the bachata, and it's something you really notice in bachatas, because the harmonic instrument of the genre is the guitar. You can add piano and synthesizer, but really the harmonies in bachata come from the guitar.

I have a piano at home and when I want to go over harmonies, I use the piano, usually when I have denser orchestrations— for example, four trumpets, four saxophones. But with bachatas, or at least with "Burbujas," which is practically a bass and a muted trumpet, I do everything on the guitar.

The "Ay ayayay" at the end of the verses is my own interpretation of the bachatero [bachata singers]. Traditional bachateros have those little cries, those unique inflections. And that was my bachatero inflection. Those kinds of things just come up when you're composing. They aren't premeditated. The lyrics are last. It's as if the melody calls the lyrics. At the time I was very influenced by Pablo Neruda, Federico García Lorca, the great poets. But mainly Neruda. At that moment, I start to work with metaphors and I finish the song. In this case, the fact that the song was sensual wasn't something I thought about when I wrote it.

Roger Zayas

The images in the song are so impactful from a literary standpoint. There is no woman you sing that song to who won't fall in love with you. They're gorgeous images, they're bucolic images. You see the lyrics. It always shocked me to go to places like Spain, which at the time became our main market, and see people in the audience singing the song top to bottom. People with tears in their eyes. This was a bachata, you know? It was the first song that I noticed generated that feeling in people: a feeling of absolute love. It was a declaration of love that was not only honest, but also sensual in a very elegant way. "Press your nose against your fishbowl," that's very clear. But it's an elegant, beautiful, pretty way of saying it.

Juan Luis Guerra

By the time I go to the studio, we can record, even if the lyrics aren't finished. Although they usually are. With "Burbujas," everything was done by the time we recorded. Once we finish the recording, the first person to listen to it outside the studio is my wife. That's when I get her approval. If she cries, it means it's a great song. For the *Bachata rosa* album, she would often mention how beautiful she found the songs to be. It was encouraging, because she thought each song was more beautiful than the last. We were all very happy, although we didn't know how far the album would go.

Roger Zayas

That album was done in multiple studios. We recorded in the Dominican Republic, in Puerto Rico, and we finally finished mixing in New York. The rhythmic bases were generally done here [in the Dominican Republic] because the merengue musicians are here. We like to record some things, especially salsa, in Puerto Rico. That's where we added the trumpets. And in New York we mix.

The problem is, Juan Luis works many things at the same time. He has that capacity to record stuff, keep it in his head, and then you suddenly see him working with different chords, and humming melodies with no lyrics. And you don't know what's coming, but you know he's in his creative process. We would always laugh at the beginning because he said he liked to compose in the bathroom because the acoustics and the natural echo were so good. So every time he went into the bathroom, we'd say, "Wow, here comes a new song. Leave him alone!"

In the recording process, in general, once we have the entire body of the song done, the last thing we add are the vocals. At the time, it was four backup singers: Marco Hernández, Adalgisa Pantaleón, Juan Luis, and me.

As background singers, we always recorded as an ensemble, always together. We weren't a professional group outside the studio. But we were all studio singers and we had chemistry between us as a vocal entity. Juan Luis is a guy who feeds from many influences. We were clear about the fact that, in music, everything has been done, and that all music is full of influences. At the time, we were listening to a lot of Huey Lewis and the News, and our vocals have that vibe that you heard in a lot of music from the '60s. We would spend all our time in the studio, so when it came time to record, whether we knew the lyrics or not, we knew the song, and Juan Luis would distribute the parts. He improvises a lot, but he's very clear about what he wants.

We still use the same system. And, yes, as we recorded, there was a certain complicity, a certain satisfaction, an implicit knowledge that we were doing something big, something special.

Amarilys Germán

That album, *Bachata rosa*, had eight singles. And everyone from our generation can sing any of those eight singles. Back in 1991, I was still a little girl, playing with dolls, so I wasn't there during the recording process. But it's the same for him today. He'll go spend hours in the studio, many times without the lyrics. And he comes back with the full song.

Roger Zayas

That song, beyond perhaps being the song that launched the [international] bachata movement, was the first one to get airplay. "Burbujas de amor" is the song that took bachata from the lower classes and dressed it in black tie. After it came "Bachata rosa" and "Estrellitas y duendes [Little stars and goblins]," and they were three amazingly good songs of great quality that people immediately began to consume. I would run into rocker friends who would tell me, "What have you done to me, for

God's sake? I used to be a rocker and now I go to bed with headphones on and listen to bachata and merengue. I can't believe it."

It was a more elegant sound, completely the opposite of what was consumed at the time. More symphonic, bigger, more complex, but still keeping the bachata essence with that muted trumpet solo and the plucked guitar. And obviously with Juan Luis's stamp, which is the vocal treatment. There were no vocal harmonies in bachata before; maybe a soloist, but not the three-, four-part vocal harmony.

Juan Luis Guerra

We knew we had something really good, but we didn't know what would happen. Everything goes so fast, you don't have time to take it in. The song simply began to grow and grow, and suddenly they were singing it in Japan and everywhere. It came from the heart. I never thought it would do one thing or the other. I simply had that harmonic base stored inside me because of those songs my uncle made me listen to in the mornings. And it just came out that way.

An important element is the way I adapted the guitar of the Beatles into bachata. The way I play guitar, mainly in this album, is with a lot of influence from George Harrison. Everyone at the time learned the Beatles' songs, and I knew "Here Comes the Sun" by heart and I thought it was the perfect pattern to adapt things to. So when I tackled bachata, I mixed the way he played with the bachata rhythm and there was something new. This new bachata is like a mix of rock and jazz, and that's what gave us a different color.

It's what happens in all movements when you mix different genres. And it's what happens when you learn how to play with a group. I learned how to play guitar by playing the Beatles. So, naturally, I've played merengue, I've played *son*, I've played bachata. At some point I'm going to infuse all of that with the music I grew up with and know by heart.

My other great influence from when I went to Berklee is Pat Metheny. Those two guitarists—George Harrison and Pat Metheny—influenced the way I play the guitar.

Amarilys Germán

Juan Luis says the Beatles played bachata and didn't know it.

Juan Luis Guerra

They have a song, "'Til There Was You," which isn't theirs, actually [it's from the musical *The Music Man*]. That song even has bongos, one of the basic instruments used to play bachata. Obviously, the bongos the Beatles use are not tuned, like ours. It's an English bongo [he laughs]. But it's a bachata all right. Listen, and you'll hear what I mean.

"Macarena"

Los Del Río
1994

PLAYERS

Alvaro de Torres: Then managing director of Warner Chappell Music Spain; currently LATAM music publishing manager for Facebook

Antonio Monge & Rafael Ruiz, Los Del Río: Artists

Carlos de Yarza: Then member of the Bayside Boys; currently professor and digital media manager at St. Thomas University

Jammin Johnny Caride: Power mixer/on-air talent, Power 96; currently programming supervisor at SBS Miami

Jesús López: Then president of BMG US Latin; currently chairman/CEO of Universal Music Latin America & Iberian Peninsula

If the 2000s had "Despacito," the 1990s had "Macarena." This most unlikely of hits by Los Del Río—two forty-something gypsy musicians from Sevilla, Spain, of little renown, even inside their own country—spent fourteen weeks at #1 on the Billboard Hot 100 in a remix version by Miami DJs the Bayside Boys.

It is the longest stint ever at #1 on the chart for a primarily non-English-language track.

But that wasn't the song's only notable feat.

The track's colorful history reads like a series of unlikely, and fortunate, events, all fueled by a catchy Spanish rumba that was remixed to acquire an even catchier dance hook, then was further remixed to become a bilingual hit at a time when bilingual hits were an aberration.

Three versions of the song—the original, the Bayside Boys' remix, and "Macarena Remix"—coexisted on the Hot 100 in 1996, the first time that had happened since April 1977 (similarly, it was the first time since the Righteous Brothers' "Unchained Melody" in 1990 that two versions of a song by the same artist coexisted on the Hot 100).

And it took the "Bayside Boys Mix" almost a full year—thirty-three weeks, to be exact—to reach #1 on the chart, the longest rise ever to the top.

Then again, nothing about "Macarena" was normal. Los Del Río wrote the track in 1992 and released it in 1993 on the small indie label Zafiro. It was a local hit in Sevilla in its original version before Zafiro ordered a remix by the Spanish band Fangoria, which was released as "Macarena River-F Mix." That version, entirely in Spanish, was the one that charted in Spain and became a hit in Latin America and the US Latin market, becoming the "Macarena" everyone in Latin America eventually danced to.

But much like "Despacito" more than twenty years later,

"Macarena" needed a bilingual remix to rise to #1 on the Hot 100 in the United States and beyond. That came courtesy not of the Justin Bieber of the time, but of two Miami DJs who called themselves the Bayside Boys and who understood the intricacies and likes and dislikes of their bilingual, bicultural city. Their "Macarena" remix was initially played on Power 96, one of the first—if not *the* first—radio stations that regularly played songs either in Spanish or with Spanish remixes.

Eventually, the Bayside Boys' retooled, bilingual "Macarena," dubbed the "Bayside Boys Mix," was a hit with American audiences, who fell prey to the same rhythm that had captivated the Spanish-speaking world once it was married to words in English.

In fact, the new "Macarena" would become the first major, successful remix on the Billboard Hot 100.

Yes, "Macarena" was an anomaly. It was danced at the 1996 Democratic National Convention, with a heady Hillary Clinton making headlines as she clapped along. In Europe, it was the soundtrack of Tour de France races and stadium soccer matches, and in the United States, it was danced during multiple sporting events, most famously at Yankee Stadium in August 1996, when Chita Rivera came to the field and led fifty thousand fans for the biggest "Macarena" dance in history. By the end of the year, it had been included in over seventy-five compilations and topped charts in dozens of countries. But in all its weirdness, it was also a precursor of things to come, opening the door for mainstream radio to play music in Spanish.

Just three years later, the Latin Explosion would sweep the world, and multiple songs with English and Spanish versions would climb the charts. "Macarena" was gone, but hardly forgotten. Gente de Zona revamped it with a new version that included Los Del Río, and in 2019, rapper Tyga released his bilingual version, also sampling the original. As for Los Del Río, they continue to tour the world, singing what may be the single most recognizable song the world over.

To date, "Macarena" remains the longest-leading, primarily non-English-language Hot 100 hit ever, and the seventh-highest ranking on the Hot 100's Greatest of All Time chart.

Antonio Monge & Rafael Ruiz

This all started in Venezuela. Gustavo Cisneros, who was the president of a big Venezuelan television network, used to come a lot to Spain. And we would go to television appearances in Venezuela. One night in 1992, we were in Gustavo Cisneros's house in Caracas, along with Carlos Andrés Pérez, who was then the president of Venezuela.

Antonio Monge

Also invited to the party was a young girl [whose name was Diana Patricia Cubillán Herrera] who studied with Tatiana Reyna, a magnificent [flamenco] dancer from Venezuela. I told Rafael, "What a beautiful thing!" And I started to say, "Dale a tu cuerpo alegría, Madalena, que tu cuerpo es pa' darle alegría y cosa buena [Give your body happiness, Madalena. Your body is made for happiness and good things]." Well, I got inspired dancing rumba.

I have a daughter named Esperanza Macarena and I thought, "I can't have a daughter with such a beautiful name and keep the name 'Madalena' in the song when her name is Macarena." Plus, we live in Sevilla and La Esperanza Macarena is the virgin of Triana and she heads the Easter processions. That's at the core of "Macarena's" great success. Sometimes we come across miracles.

I came up with everything during that party. We went back to the hotel and I had the chorus practically done in my mind. In my room, the other ingredients came to me: "Macarena sueña con el corte inglés [Macarena dreams with el corte inglés] . . . tiene un novio llamado Vittorino [she has a boyfriend called Vittorino]." Next morning, during rehearsals at the hotel with the team and the musicians, we started to rehearse it.

When we returned from Venezuela, it was December and we were in the middle of Christmas parties, and we got together with a bunch of Spanish artist friends at the farm of a great friend, Manolo Prado. Our "sister" Rocío Jurado was there, and I think that's where we sang it for the first time in public. Rocío said, "You've made a great shot."

We recorded it in Sevilla in this famous flamenco studio, Estudios Bola. That's where they record much of the flamenco that goes out to the world. We had an out-of-this-world [person] called Manolito Soler [Soler died in 2003], a flamenco bailaor—he played the guitar, he sang, he had a tremendous capacity and knowledge of rhythm. I took the song, practically finished, and they did the arrangements. The "Ay!" that comes at the end of the phrases, that's very typical of Sevilla. It's almost like a greeting for us.

We premiered "Macarena" on Andalusian television during the Sevilla Fair. We could tell that something was happening with the song. The Sevilla Fair is made up of 1,300 to 1,400 casetas [tents built to host attendees, including family and friends as well as visitors] and every year, some one hundred sevillana albums are released [which get played in different casetas]. So, what happens? "Macarena" comes out and all 1,400 casetas, the entire Sevilla Fair, is playing "Macarena." It didn't stop. Cadena Ser named it the song of the summer, and radio stations, too. In 1994 the "Macarena" revolution took us out of Spain. We went to Ecuador, Lebanon, Mexico, Egypt. They danced it everywhere in the world. We had released it on Zafiro, a small label that was purchased by BMG Ariola. When that happened, the song went international.

Jesús López

Los Del Río released the song in 1993, but nothing happened. But in the summer of 1994, it begins to become a hit in Spain and it remains a summer hit in Spain, although it wasn't the biggest song, either. At the time, I was the president of BMG US Latin and Mexico, based in Miami.

One day I went to spend the weekend in Mexico with an artist who was playing a show in Querétaro. We ended up having dinner at a Friday's. Suddenly, the "Macarena" played, and the waiters stopped what they were doing and started to dance. Not the "Macarena" dance. A dance. I knew the "Macarena." Not only did I know it, but I was one of those record executives who thought he knew everything and who had said this would never work outside Spain because it talks about Vittorino, el corte inglés. Things we understand in Spain, but wouldn't be understood in the United States or Mexico.

I was surprised at what I saw. And the next night, I had a show with Joaquín Sabina [who is Spanish] in Guadalajara, and I asked him, "What's up with 'La Macarena'?" And he said, "Yeah, last year it played in all the gas stations and dives in the country."

I went back to our offices in Mexico City and told my marketing director, "I want you to do a test for me. Now that it's spring break, make sure this song plays in all the clubs in Playa del Carmen, Cancún, and the like, and I want to know if people react or not." Next day in Miami, I said the same thing to my marketing director there, but I asked him to test the market in Puerto Rico and the Dominican Republic. A month, two months later, "Macarena" started to play on some radio stations in Mexico and the Caribbean. At that moment I thought we needed a dance, otherwise it wouldn't work. I hired a choreographer who did a remix and brought the dancers over, and they invented the "Macarena" dance in my office at BMG.

Los Del Río

[Zafiro] was a very poor label. A very little label. When BMG and Ariola realized what they had, they started to negotiate with our manager. And next thing we knew, we were on BMG Ariola. There was no video until the new label came in and made several videos. There was one with twelve young girls: one from China, one from Spain, one from Mexico. From several countries. Logically, when a record label sees they have a song with so much pull, everybody gets on board.

Jammin Johnny Carlde

I was a full-time DJ and mixer for Power 96 in Miami [96.5 FM]. Power 96 was the soundtrack of South Florida. Everybody wanted to be part of it, and we always stayed tuned into what the community was about. And the community was Hispanic. Back then, either you only played music in Spanish or you only played English. I like to say that Power was the station that made the crossover into English and Spanish music.

I had a gig as a DJ on Sundays at Baja Beach Club in Coconut Grove for a Latin night I had put together for the salseros and merengueros [salsa and merengue dancers], but I'd also play some freestyle music. And I started to notice that people would come up and ask me about a song called "Macarena." I had no idea. Macaroni, Macarena? I don't know what the heck that is. When I asked around, they told me it was a Spanish song they were playing at a Spanish club in Miami Beach. I couldn't find it, so I looked in my record pool. I used to get all kinds of music—salsa, merengue. But they'd always send us what we DJs called Frisbees, because we would throw them out and never use them again. But I'm a hoarder, and, sure enough, among all that I found Los Del Río's "Macarena." I went to my gig on Sunday, and I played the song in the middle of the set. And all at once, the dance floor just cleared out and everybody started doing the dance. And the people who didn't know it, they looked around, they got it, and they started doing it, too. I said, "Wait, wait. What is this? Electric Slide in Spanish?" Truth is, I had never seen anything like it. You're in a club, there are all these couples dancing merengue and salsa together, and all of a sudden the dance floor opens and they do a line dance? It really struck me. The following week, I was working at another club with Kid Curry, the programmer for Power 96.

It was one-thirty in the morning and I said, "Kid, I want to play this Spanish record on the radio."

He said, "You're gonna play a Spanish record on Power 96?"

I said, "Yeah. Check it out."

And I play the song and the same thing happens. It was like the bubonic plague. The dance floor clears out, people fall in line, like an army, and they start to do that little dance. The ones who didn't know it, they learn it on the spot. And the boss looks at me and says, "What the hell was that?"

I told him, "Bro, I don't know, but something's going on with that song."

Kid says, "We gotta talk to [station head] Frank Walsh and see what we do."

Los Del Río

A lot of artists released versions. Those remixes are what gave it such strength. Everyone was behind that song. We played concerts in Germany with Montserrat Caballé. Then the German soccer team won the European Cup, they were greeted back in Germany with "Macarena." According to SGAE (Spain's General Society of Authors), there are more than 120 million copies of "Macarena" sold. It's what every artist wants: to make something the world can enjoy.

Jesús López

They did the remix in Miami. It was very important, because it gave it new life and a much more Latin touch than it initially had.

Jammin Johnny Caride

Next day, Frank hears the song and says, "You got seventy-two hours to come up with a remix that can be played on the radio." I had my own label, Bayside Records, with Mike "In the Night" Triay and Carlos de Yarza, and we were producing and making records with several artists. I went to Mike and Carlos and said, "This is our opportunity to break into radio with a song that's going to be massive." We decided to keep the essentials of the guys singing and get a female voice to answer them in English. But we said, "Let's do it Hialeah style. 'Hello, my name ees Macarena, come dance with meee.'" Carlos said he had the perfect person. He wrote her part, she came to the studio, recorded it, they produced it and called and said, "It's ready to go."

Carlos de Yarza

In the early '90s Mike and I had a recording studio and we had a relationship with Power 96, which at the time was playing local artists, which was amazing for us. They would come to us [and ask us to remix tracks for the station]. They would send us songs to toy with so they could sound different from Y-100.

At the time "Macarena" gets into the studio, I'm looking at this like another Power 96 thing. I tell Mike, "Let me listen to this song." I'm a lyricist. This girl is not getting her voice out. Let's give her a voice. In like fifteen minutes I came up with this ridiculous lyric. And I called a girl we had met on another project, called Patty Alfaro. She is the original voice you hear on this recording. I called her up and I said, "I have this ridiculous song. Can you please just come into the studio and become this character? This is probably going to Power. They'll play it twice and that will be the end of it." She came to the studio, and in two, three hours, we put it on a DAT [digital audiotape] and we sent it to Power.

Jammin Johnny Caride

I took it back to Power. Cox on the Radio [the highly rated show helmed by DJ Don Cox, who died in 2003] was on and Frank said, "Play it now." What can I say? People instantly started calling, as if we were giving away $1,000. They were saying, "Play it again, play it again." In less than a week, we went from being nothings to overnight celebrities. They started calling us the Bayside Boys. We had to start printing CDs and CD covers and with the little money we had, FedExing them to radio stations all over the country. Labels wanted to sign us. Until one day

BMG called and said, "Guys, we're flattered that you worked on our project, but you have no rights to sell this to anyone but us."

Carlos de Yarza

The next phone call we got was from RCA in-house counsel.

"Bayside Music. This is Carlos. Can I help you?"

"Hi. Are you the guys that did the Macarena thing?"

"Yes."

"Give us your attorney's number."

That was the entire phone call. That was a week in. Because Power cloned the DAT tape and sent it to a bunch of other Power stations in the Latin pockets and they started banging it as well. And that got RCA's attention. Here's the story that I got later: RCA's original intent was to cease and desist on the song. But apparently there was one guy running through the offices, saying, "No, we can't kill the song!" And everybody else is trying to shut it down.

Alvaro de Torres

I got a call in 1995 and they tell me that "Macarena" has been redone without authorization by some Miami DJs. We found out what it was, they send us the copies, and we see that the song has been changed; they added a girl. All that was done without our permission. So the label came to an agreement that allowed them to do it as long as BMG had the rights, and we signed [a contract for] a derivative work from "Macarena" that we called "Macarena Bayside Boys Remix," where they had a writer's share as adapters or coauthors.

Carlos de Yarza

We went to see our lawyer [David Bercuson] and he said, "They want to give you a go-away fee." From my perspective it was more than zero and I truly didn't think this thing would do anything. We signed the deal memo and I went back to work. It was a regular day.

Then RCA calls again and says, "Can you guys put something together and do shows for us?"

And from the summer of 1995 to maybe November, December, we started doing a ton of small gigs—me, Mike, and Patty. But the song started dying out. Until radio station WKTU opened up in New York [in February 1996], and they put "Macarena" on heavy rotation. And then things got very, very interesting. Patty didn't want to tour anymore, so we asked Carla Vanessa Ramirez to go on the road with us.

We start getting booked everywhere and the song really starts climbing the *Billboard* charts. We are seriously in support of this thing. We didn't sleep for like six months. And our agent would call every week and say, "Hey, guys, we're number forty-six this week. We're thirty-five this week. We're Top Ten." And every time I would giggle. I couldn't believe this ridiculous song.

The apex was the summer of 1996, when the song hit #1. We went on the *Oprah* show and the same week the US [Olympic] Gymnastics Team used the song. Everything just hit in that summer of 1996. But it was entirely due to the fact that New York played that song.

Los Del Río

We played the Super Bowl in New Orleans. Everybody was singing "Macarena." The gymnastics team danced the "Macarena" during the Olympic Games in Atlanta. Italy and Real Madrid played the seventh European Cup in Amsterdam. The Italians took an Italian singer to perform before the game, and nothing happened. We sang the song from the other goal, and the entire stadium—Italians and Spaniards—started singing "Macarena."

Alvaro de Torres

There were dozens of versions, in every language and every style you can imagine. But the global success came from the Bayside Boys' remix. Thanks to that, the song became #1 around the world. It was pure success. The biggest song I've ever worked.

Carlos de Yarza

We really pushed to get this Bayside Boys thing out there as a dance group. We weren't making money from the song, but we were making a mint from the shows. They gave me a very small percentage of the lyrics, and I still get royalties as a writer from ASCAP. If I hadn't been so young, I would have asked for more. But I understand it is what it is. It's a different lifetime. It's okay. It pays for my vacations.

Antonio Monge

I wrote the song, but we've been lifetime partners, so I also gifted it to Rafael. He's the coauthor with me, and both of us collect the royalties. We realize the royalties are probably not what they should be, because the song went to #1 in many countries where we don't get anything. But God knows what he does. And he gave us this marvelous gift of having a hit song in every corner of the world. The chorus of the song is so easy: "Give your body happiness." It's such an important thing that should be said daily. And we see the repercussion all these years later. In every concert, in every wedding, in every First Communion, people dance "Macarena." Never can you imagine that the president of the United States will use your song for his campaign. This "Macarena" just went everywhere, and even today, little five-, six-year-olds will stop us on the street and sing "Macarena."

It has allowed us to take happiness everywhere, to make people happier in this complicated world. That's why we're here.

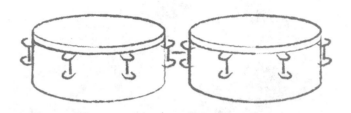

"Amor prohibido"
Selena
1994

PLAYERS

A.B. Quintanilla: Producer, songwriter

Abraham Quintanilla: Selena's father, manager

Chris Pérez: Musician, Selena's ex-husband

José Behar: Then president of EMI Music Latin; now manager

Pete Astudillo: Songwriter

On March 31, 1995, Selena Quintanilla Pérez left her home at 9:00 a.m. with plans to go to the recording studio to lay down vocals for a demo. Instead, at 11:49 a.m., she stumbled into the lobby of a Days Inn motel, clutching her chest, a trail of blood behind her. "Help me, help me!" she shouted as she collapsed to the floor. "I've been shot."

By 1:00 p.m., she was dead, just weeks shy of her twenty-fourth birthday, murdered by the former president of her fan club.

Sudden, tragic death has the bittersweet effect of turning stars into icons and younger stars into legends.

Selena was already on her way to becoming both.

A charismatic performer who possessed a distinctive voice—both husky and sweet—and was intuitively aware of the requirements of stardom (she designed all her outfits, including those now-legendary bustiers, and choreographed all her dance moves), Selena had pushed Tejano music into mainstream awareness. With only two years of a major recording contract under her belt, she'd placed five #1 singles on Billboard's Hot Latin Songs chart.

The month before, she'd picked up her first Grammy Award on national television, and her crossover album was almost done.

Dreaming of You wasn't released until almost five months after her death, but it still debuted at #1 on the Billboard 200 chart, a first for a Latin female act. Ironically, only Jennifer Lopez would equal this feat years later, after her role in the film *Selena* jump-started her singing career.

Dreaming of You's success notwithstanding, if there is a song—and an album—that laid out the before and after in Selena's career, it would be "Amor prohibido (Forbidden love)," the story of lovers torn by social class divisions. A peppy cumbia, it followed a different kind of crossover path for Latin music, one that went from the United States into Latin America, instead of the other way round.

Still, while Selena's music traveled internationally, her real influence lies in her impact within the United States.

The album *Amor prohibido* was a milestone, too. Released on March 13, 1994, via Capitol Latin, it also included "Bidi

bidi bom bom," "No me queda más (I have nothing else)," and "Fotos y recuerdos (Photos and memories)."

The set, produced by her brother, A.B. Quintanilla, revolutionized Tejano music in the '90s, fusing the genre with blends of hip-hop, ranchera, cumbia, and electronic beats.

On June 11, 1994, *Amor prohibido* became Selena's first album to hit #1 on the Top Latin Albums chart, where it stayed for twenty nonconsecutive weeks.

Two months before, the album debuted at #1 on the Regional Mexican Album chart, dated April 9, 1994, where it remained for ninety-seven nonconsecutive weeks—the most weeks at #1 for an album overall in the history of the chart.

In addition, it was Selena's first chart entry on the Billboard 200, where it peaked at #29, remaining a total of twenty-three weeks on the chart.

Selena's importance went way beyond the charts. Because she was a homegrown star, she was widely recognized both by Latin and non-Latin fans. In a world (still) of telegenic, imported Latin pop stars, Selena was an anomaly; bilingual and bicultural, not only did she look like her fans, she *was* like them. That relatability was transformative for Latin pop culture.

Thanks to Selena, for the first time, perhaps ever, US-born Latinas had a role model they could aspire to be. Two generations later, Selena's impact is still tangible. Dozens of prominent figures—from Becky G to Jennifer Lopez, Leslie Grace, and Selena Gomez—point to Selena as their direct influence. Selena's legacy has been fundamental in creating a new movement of US-born Latin artists. Today, twenty-five years after her death, they are collectively reaping success and still naming her as the precursor of their achievements.

José Behar

When I opened EMI Latin on February 20, 1989, one of the first things I did was go to the Tejano Music Awards. I came from CBS Records, and back then nobody left CBS. But I decided I wanted to leave for EMI because I didn't want to be an A&R guy my entire life. Joe Smith was then the president/CEO of Capitol EMI. I go to Texas for the Tejano awards. And I come back and Joe Smith says, "How did it go in Texas?" And I said, "I think I found the next Gloria Estefan."

When I signed Selena, I never signed her to sell Tejano music. Everyone says she's the Tejano queen. But she was just from Texas. At the end of the day, when you listen to songs like "Amor prohibido," "No me queda más," that's not Tejano music, because if that were the case, it would have never worked in Mexico.

Abraham Quintanilla

My grandmother was from Nueva Rosita, Coahuila, Mexico. Back in those years in Mexico there was no middle class. Either you had money or you didn't have any. My grandmother, her maiden name was Concepción Castro. They called her Conchita. She was the maid of the Calderón family, a prominent Mexican family of that time in that area of Mexico. Later on, we found out that their origins were from Spain. But my grandmother was the maid of the family. The Calderón family had four sons. One of them was Humberto.

Humberto and my grandmother, the maid, were in love. One day, the brothers go hunting and Humberto was accidentally shot.

When he died at the age of twenty-three, my grandmother was three months' pregnant by him. And as soon as he died, the mother, the matron of the Calderón family, booted her out of the home. "Vamos, vamos, váyase [Come on, go, leave]!" My grandmother and her parents walked from Nueva Rosita, Coahuila, all the way to Edna, Texas, and my mother was born in Edna, Texas. By the way, my mother was the only child that Conchita ever had.

We never knew any of this until my grandmother told me the story. They booted her out of the house because there was a social status issue. She's a maid and these people had money. That's why the song is called "Amor prohibido": two social classes.

That's the story I'm telling A.B. and the whole bus when we're traveling. And that's where the song came from. Later on Pete [Astudillo] and A.B. got together and wrote the song. It was a forbidden love because they came from different social classes.

Pete Astudillo*

Selena was always about teamwork. I wrote "Amor prohibido" with A.B. I always wanted to write a song that spoke about relationships, especially between people of different social classes. It's not really about money, but about love. Basically, that was the song. Selena really identified with it [. . .] as a person who came from a humble family, and who reached a very important position.

---

* Pete Astudillo was not interviewed for this book. His words come from spoken liner notes for Selena's album *Momentos íntimos*, Capitol Latin, 2004.

Abraham Quintanilla

My sister Gloria was always very inquisitive about where we came from. Years later, she and her husband went to Nueva Rosita, Coahuila, and started searching the birth records and the church records and all that, and finally located some of the Calderón family. But now it's four generations later. My sister Gloria was armed with only one photograph of Humberto. They give her this address and she goes and knocks on their door. Can you imagine a stranger coming to your door and saying, "Hey, we're related!"

And, of course, they didn't accept that. The fourth-generation Calderóns who lived there didn't even let her in the house. But they gave her the name and address of another one of the relatives. So Gloria goes to the other address and this other family was very welcoming. They invited her in and Gloria started telling them the story and she showed them the picture and they said, "Ah, we have a copy of that!"

They told her Humberto had died at twenty-three. And the brother who had mental problems burned the Calderón family home, burned it down. And they saved one chest. And inside the chest there was this photo of Humberto and the last letter he wrote to his mother, the matriarch. He said, "I was in San Antonio and Dr. Gonzalez couldn't do nothing for me, so they moved me to a New Orleans hospital and they're going to operate on me tomorrow. I'm very sick, I don't know if I'm going to make it." And he didn't make it.

He died of gangrene. The bullet wound poisoned his blood and he died at the age of twenty-three.

So Gloria tells them, "We're related. My mother is Humberto's daughter." And they gave her some of the things that were in the chest: the last letter he wrote from the hospital in New Orleans and the family seal. They were Spaniards from Spain. My sister told them, "I have a brother named Abraham Quintanilla, Hector, Eduardo, Isaac, and a sister called Yolanda." But she never mentioned anything about Selena.

A.B. Quintanilla*

A lot of pressure was on me on the first album and it did very well, and they said, "Okay, we'll give him a shot on the second album." And from there it started taking off and taking off and taking off. The recording process was cool. 'Cause I was given total freedom to do whatever I felt I had to do. With every album Selena had come out in the Latin market, it reached more and more markets. It happened because there was extensive work done on the music to reach certain regions. Once we took over Texas, I wanted the United States. I started kinda disguising our music with sounds and textures. It's like sending subliminal messages. Like, if you listen to banda music, it was like hiding banda behind a cumbia. Once I started hiding things, studying groups in Mexico, I got her into Mexico. I wasn't happy with just Mexico. I wanted Central America, so I started studying Central America. Cumbia is on downbeats and salsa is on upbeats. So what a lot of people don't know, on "Amor prohibido" I switched the cowbell to a salsa cowbell. That salsa cowbell is tuned worldwide, it's tuned to the same key. By doing that, I busted the market open for her, so that everybody accepted the music. I wanted to know why she couldn't hit that #1 spot on Billboard, *until the one day that it did happen, and "Amor prohibido" went to #1. So we were kind of handicapped with the style of music we play, and to go to #1 that was a big thing.*

---

*   Quotes taken from a video interview with *Billboard*, "Remembering Selena: Q&A with A.B. Quintanilla III," Billboard.com, April 1, 2015, https://www.billboard.com/video/remembering-selena-qa-with-ab-quintanilla -iii-6517049.

José Behar

They would send us demos and then they would send us the recording, and at the end of the day we made a great team. The label, Selena, Abraham. Pete Astudillo was the lyricist and A.B. was an amazing producer and did the arrangements.

Selena was at the Sheraton Universal and I went to see her and she played music for me.

I thought it was a smash. The lyrics are insane. The lyrics are insane. It's a masterpiece. I had to decide between "Bidi bidi bom bom" and "Amor prohibido," and I chose "Amor prohibido." "Amor prohibido" speaks to the people, to the masses, to everyone at some point in their lives. Either directly or indirectly. These are lyrics that stand the test of time. It's as relevant, if not more relevant than ever. Things don't change. And I just think she sings it so beautifully, too. Selena never had a voice lesson and never had a choreographer work with her. And you listen to "Amor prohibido," and you are blown away even more.

Chris Pérez*

The "Amor prohibido" video was filmed in Joshua Tree National Park. It's basically out in the middle of nowhere. We didn't stay very far from the location where we shot the video. It was a really exciting time. We weren't used to doing videos on that scale.

When she was picking her clothes to do her video to get ready to fly out, I remember her going through the closet. There was no shortage of clothes or shoes with her. I remember her turning around and looking at my side of the closet. She started going through some of my shirts. And sure enough she pulled some out and ended up

---

*   From spoken liner notes for Selena's album *Momentos íntimos*.

wearing one of those red shirts I'd bought at the mall. And in that video, when she's wearing the long-sleeved red shirt and she has it tied at the bottom, that's one of my shirts.

Abraham Quintanilla

I heard the song after they recorded it. I liked it. How many families have gone through an experience like that? People go through these things in life.

Years later, when Selena was killed, the media in Mexico went crazy. And when they heard Selena Quintanilla and Abraham Quintanilla, these people [the Calderóns] put two and two together.

So here they come. We met them for the first time. They came to Corpus Christi after Selena passed away. Selena would have been the great-granddaughter. I didn't tell them the song was about them. But I'm sure they figured it out. It could be a telenovela.

But at that time, I was so involved in the business end of the group that I missed a lot of things. And believe it or not, when Selena got killed, it erased a lot of things from my mind.

"La tierra del olvido"
Carlos Vives
1995

PLAYERS

Carlos Vives: Artist, composer

Egidio Cuadrado: Accordionist

Iván Benavides: Composer

Mayte Montero: Gaita player

Throughout the 1980s, Colombia went through profound social, economic, and cultural change, buffeted by drug wars and a civil war between the government and guerrillas.

The unrest, coupled with what was seen as lack of representation and rampant corruption, led to the signing of a new Colombian constitution in 1991, which recognized the country as a "culturally and ethnically diverse" nation, whose cultural and natural riches were to be protected.

It was during this time of newfound patriotism, of looking at the familiar with pride instead of contempt, that Carlos Vives rose to stardom.

An actor and singer, he'd gained some local success as a soap-opera actor and as a pop balladeer. Until 1991, when he played the role of Rafael Escalona in *Escalona*, a television series based on the life of the fabled vallenato composer.

Vallenato, the accordion-based music of Colombia's Caribbean coast, known for the troubadour spirit of its lyrics, had long been the music of the masses, often shunned by the upper classes and trendy media.

Vives, who came from an upper-middle-class family and loved rock en español, was at first glance an unlikely ambassador. Except he was perfect.

He was born in Santa Marta in the Caribbean, in a home where all kinds of Latin music was played: Mexican, Cuban, Puerto Rican, Spanish ballads, Latin American folk. But the Vives family had deep connections to Colombian music in general and close links to vallenato and cumbia in particular, and it was common for the singers and musicians of those genres to visit and perform in the family home. That contact would plant the early seeds of what would become Vives's musical base, and his portrayal of Escalona shone new light on the composer. More importantly, his contemporary take on classic vallenato sparked a sudden broader interest in the music.

Vives had the credibility of his pedigree, of his knowledge of the music, and of his band, La Provincia, which included accordionist Egidio Cuadrado and gaitera Mayte Montero (the gaita is an indigenous flute). But Vives also had edge. As a rocker, he couldn't help himself. He inserted drums and electric guitar into *Clásicos de La Provincia* (*Classics from La Provincia*), an album of vallenato standards recorded in 1993. The set was a resounding success, leading many to believe Vives would come up with a sequel.

Instead, along with La Provincia, he dug deep. He and his band holed up at a farm, where for weeks they worked on a new blueprint for Colombia's distinctive beats, one that married the most traditional of folk rhythms and genres with a contemporary edge; the Caribbean and the mountains; the tropics and the cold; rock and cumbia (a mix of African, Spanish, and Native beats and instrumentation born on Colombia's Caribbean coast); North and South; music for the masses and music for musicians.

It was all built on the undeniable foundation of Colombia, from its instruments and its rhythmic patterns to the land itself—wild and untamed and breathtaking and diverse and forgotten for so long.

La tierra del olvido (*The land of the forgotten*)—the album and the song that gives it its name—would forever change the course of Colombian music. It introduced vallenato to the world; the genre, to this day, remains broadly fused into all kinds of Latin music. It opened the door for Colombian artists to become global superstars; every Colombian star, from Shakira to Maluma and J Balvin, owes a debt of gratitude to Vives. And the song spawned an entire new musical movement, tropi-pop, that blend of pop and rock with Colombian tropical beats that would become the signature of artists from Juanes to Fonseca.

As for Vives, he remains Colombia's most authentic musical ambassador, a man deeply vested in mining and preserving his country's heritage—from vallenato and beyond—by making music that's eminently, joyfully commercial.

It all started with this one song, crafted on the outskirts of Bogotá by rockers, folk instrumentalists, and even a British producer, bound by the common desire to find greatness by looking within.

Carlos Vives

It was 1994 and we had created a new kind of format for our "Tropicality" when we recorded *Clásicos de La Provincia* [the 1993 album in which Vives reimagined classic vallenato songs with contemporary flair]. Not only did it trigger pride in vallenato, but it was also a new sound for our songs. That's why that album—*Clásicos de La Provincia*—is so important in my life. But I was facing a next album. And I couldn't continue to just record classic vallenatos. Or at least, the next release couldn't be another album of classic vallenatos; no more songs by old composers of the time. I was faced with composing. I was faced with understanding what we'd accomplished with that first album. The first thing I had learned about vallenato was that it was the son of cumbia, and it opened up to a much bigger universe that touched all our Colombian culture. It was a broader musical DNA that I called "La tierra del olvido [The land of the forgotten]." It was for me to find myself with my roots. I came from recording ballads, and I was searching for my identity. In a way I was forgetting my land, and that's why I called the album and the song "La tierra del olvido."

I saw myself reflected in that album cover, where I stand in front of the Caribbean and at the foot of the Sierra Nevada de Santa Marta [one of the highest coastal ranges in the world at 18,700 feet], the "Colombian Tibet," and home to our indigenous Tayrona cultures.

Iván Benavides

Carlos had done very well with *Clásicos de La Provincia*, which was an album of covers of songs by vallenato troubadours. He was building his team, and he knew to surround himself with very good people. We knew him slightly. I worked as a song-writer for a lot of people, and Carlos knew me because I was part of that generation.

Gabriel García Márquez used to say that the great Caribbean begins in the South of the United States. That the Caribbean culturally begins there, and that New Orleans has much more in common with the Caribbean than with New York.

And, due to one of those accidents of destiny, we were able to bring together an incredibly creative team. He changed a few elements in the band, brought in producer and arranger Richard Blair [who had worked with Peter Gabriel], guitarist Teto Ocampo, Mayte Montero, who played gaita with Totó la Momposina. Suddenly you had an interesting laboratory of work.

Carlos Vives

The song was born from working with my team of La Provincia. Iván Benavides was in my production team and told me, "Lock yourself up somewhere and write." I had written romantic poems when I was young, little school songs. I came from singing ballads by balladeers and then I'd done vallenato classics my father and my uncles taught me. And now I was facing this "Go and write."

A friend had a farm in Santandercito, which is not far south of Bogotá. It's a very beautiful place with exuberant nature. This friend lent us a house and I went there with what was my band at the time, to put together ideas, arrange music. So we went to this farm.

It was crazy. At the same time, I was producing an under-ground television program called *La tele*. It was a wild comedy show, and we were taping the episodes in a studio near the farm [while] we were producing the album. So it was a very crazy, extremely creative moment, where I was working both music and television, and that's where I knew I had the feeling of "La tierra del olvido." Especially because in my work at the time I was beginning to open up a universe of local music: of patterns, percussions, different sounds from what was being heard at the time. So this was a not wanting to forget, a remembering to look within instead of outside.

Iván Benavides

[Look] with self-recognition and cultural identity. [Recording together] allowed us to recognize each other in our local languages and also speak with the world. When all was said and done, we were a bunch of young rockers who loved salsa and folk music. That allowed us to find ourselves. Because we spoke a lot before sitting down to write. So, we had the rock side and the folk side. El Papa [bass player Luis Ángel "El Papa" Pastor] was kind of the translator and Carlos guided the boat. We'd spent all day creating music in that laboratory. I spent a lot of time sitting in a hammock. When you're a composer, silence precedes creation, and you need a lot of silence. The song flowed in a few minutes, both lyrics and music.

Carlos Vives

You know what it feels like to sit in front of a blank paper. Imagine the challenge I had to make songs that said "Carlos Vives!" It was exciting, but I had that notion of recovering what was mine. That nostalgia made the song. I felt nostalgic and I had to write that. "Yo siempre voy a regresar a ti, como la luna que alumbra los caminos [I'll always return to you, like the moon that lights the paths]." We started with the music. I sometimes have words written out that I put music to. But generally I have a sound that I want that song to have. For example, a song has to begin in a very specific way. And, generally speaking, when you have the beginning defined, it's very easy to come up with the rest. That little piece of DNA in a verse, that if you listen to it enough, you know it will be the same verse that will lead to the pre-chorus and then to a joyous chorus, and then you'll probably have a little rap or some other variant.

I hadn't done it before, but I had a clear idea of how the song should sound. I knew I wanted it to be a romantic song, a song that would straddle traditional Caribbean music we all know and the coast and vallenato. I knew I didn't want to make a classic vallenato, which is what I had just done. I was looking for a new song, and it has the style of a new song.

I felt I was writing an analogy of how I felt. I feel like a bird from that place. I feel like a rock from that place. I feel I'm part of that nature. That's something vallenatos gave back to me. That's why "La tierra del olvido" has a vallenato element. But it has also something from Cuba, it has elements from our traditional ballads, it has what was pop music at the time, and I wanted to incorporate all that, with our roots as the base. So, what I wanted was very clear, and that allowed me to quickly arrive at that first song of an album for which I would write several songs. But that song is that nostalgia that inspires the album.

Iván Benavides

I spoke a lot with Carlos. My songs tend to be darker. And Carlos kept saying we had to find something more hopeful. And talking so much about the Magdalena River [in Colombia] and the Mississippi River, we started to think about the periphery. Although the song is a love song, the entire subtext takes us to a deep Colombia. A forgotten Colombia. I've always been in love with the peripheries. We were able to bring two very beautiful things together. It's a love song, and in Latin love songs, typically it's the woman who waits. In this song, the man waits: "This is how I await your return to the forgotten land." The man shows his vulnerability, and in the forgotten land he pays homage to that deep Colombia. It's also a nod to Gabriel García Márquez. In *Love in the Time of Cholera*, there's a phrase that makes reference to that Colombia.

Carlos Vives

We had a recording console at the farm. We would get together in the afternoons. You always kind of laze around in the mornings. I would sit with my notebook in my room and I was producing the television show. People would go play soccer, or to the pool or to walk around the mountains. And around six in the afternoon, when it started to get dark, we would all get together. We'd turn on the equipment. We had our engineer there, and Iván and I would say, "Here is the song." We'd sing it with guitar and voice first. Then the bass would get it and start playing. Then the percussion. And we would start to record that first demo right there at the farm.

Egidio Cuadrado

Carlos and I had worked together since *Escalona* [the 1991 television series where Vives played vallenato legend Rafael Escalona, and which spawned two companion albums]. *La tierra del olvido*, we started to work on at a farm that belonged to Dr. Belisario González. That's when my brother Carlos began to arrange music in his style. And that song, "La tierra del olvido," was done between my brother Carlos and Iván Benavides. It was a song with a lot of accordion. I had a lot of solos, and a lot of playing with the guitar and Mayte's gaita. It's one of my compadre Carlos's favorite songs, and mine, too. I work on my accordion arrangements, and then with all La Provincia, including my compadre Carlos, we work, we add, we take out.

Mayte Montero

I was already part of the band because we had gone on tour with *Clásicos de La Provincia* That's when I came in. It had been a couple of years and it was time to do a new album. *La tierra del olvido* was the best recording and production experience I had with an album because we didn't work in a recording studio. We went to a farm. And everything was very relaxed and devoted 100 percent to making music. We had a recording console to work whatever flowed, like a jam, very free.

Carlos would write stuff with Iván Benavides. We'd do the songs late in the day, when we were already rested. We were up late, because musicians are sleepwalkers. It was, "Go outside, sleep in the hammock, eat whatever you want." Everything was so relaxed. Each of us would find their own little corner, but when it came time to get together, we each had to bring a proposal based on the inspiration we got from the experience the night before. It wasn't the usual system of "Here's the producer, here's the song, and this is what you have to play." This was amazing because every time I felt my gaita had a place, well, I simply began to create the arrangements on my own, and when we were together, I'd bring them in. It was the first time in a recording session that I could say, "This is where I want my gaita to go."

And those songs that I didn't know as well because the spaces were still being created, Carlos or the composer would suggest a place for the gaita. That's how the album as a whole came together, and it was unforgettable. It's been the only album I've done that was 100 percent inspired by liberty.

Carlos Vives

We also wrote "Pa' Mayte" ["For Mayte," a song dedicated expressly to Mayte Montero] at the same farm, around that time, working with Mayte, who had come in as the gaitera of La Provincia. She was the first female gaita player in the history of the music. Mayte brought us champetas [another Colombian folk rhythm]. At the time we were listening to champeta and El General and the movement that gave birth to reggactón. Mayte was from Cartagena and she inspired this song. I wrote it with Iván and with Teto, and it became her anthem. But everything worked that way. We turned on the power at 6:00 p.m. and just worked on it from there until it was pretty late.

Mayte Montero

There was commitment, of course. The commitment to create. All ideas were welcome. And they were really well welcomed. It was fantastic. It was the only one we did that way, outside in the open, with the sounds around us, without a time limit, with every idea welcome to the table.

[In "La tierra del olvido"] Carlos and Iván were flowing and it was one of those songs where they explored a new fusion. It starts with a vallenato and then you blend [other things] and arrive at a new vallenato: Carlos Vives's vallenato. It was like a workshop with people from different parts of Colombia. We had the cachacos [people from Bogotá] and the costeños [people from the coast]. I had never really spoken with Guajiros [people from the state of Guajira, at the northeastern tip of the country]. As a costeña [from Cartagena, on the Caribbean coast], we have many commonalities but also many differences. Carlos was very samario [from Santa Marta, some two hours west of Cartagena] but with a very Caribbean vibe. And we all were into vallenato, which is listened to on all the coasts. But really, it was a coming together of cachacos and costeños, a very Colombian encounter. The cachacos brought to the table the rock element, and we came with the folk, the accordion, the caja vallenata, the cumbia. All those rhythms. It was like we found each other. I remember Iván sitting in a hammock with his guitar. He'd sing the song for me and say, "Mayte, let's start to play your sound here with the guitar to see if it works."

Carlos Vives

The Carlos Vives sound is the result of taking the ancient percussion used in the cumbia and its offspring and reformatting it for electric guitars, keyboards, and drums. This became a new sound, the Carlos Vives, which is born from traditional music. It's a sound I'd already inserted into the old vallenato songs. We had a new way of playing the drums, electric guitars, and keyboard that came from cumbia and vallenato patterns [traditional vallenato is not played with drums, only with percussion]. In "La gota fría" ["The cold drop," Vives's previous hit], we had devised a way to include electric guitars. Mind you, "La gota fría" is a song that had been recorded hundreds of times before I recorded it. But the way we did it allowed the song to grow in new ways. So, I knew what [sound and rhythmic] patterns I wanted to use, but I had to find the song.

Iván Benavides

The other very interesting thing about the song was the battle Carlos waged to make an album with complete, independent creative liberty, but backed by commercial muscle. A song like "La tierra del olvido" wouldn't be allowed today. I timed it recently, and it has over fifty seconds of accordion. Today they wouldn't let you have more than fifteen seconds. The song kicks off with a descending chromatic bass line, which is something that doesn't exist in folk. It exists in pop and rock in songs like "Dear Prudence" and songs by Charly García [an Argentine singer-songwriter, musician, and producer]. But Carlos and I were superfans of Argentine rock.

Carlos Vives

Iván as a producer was like a point of reference that was very close to the British. He was close to Richard Blair, who worked with Peter Gabriel and Totó la Momposina [a widely respected Colombian folksinger]. The musicians I hung out with also hung out with the British and Iván was an important piece.

And the guitarist was Ernesto [Teto] Ocampo, one of the most important anthropologists in Colombia. He was my guitarist for a short time because he was a professor and his thing was anthropology. I feed off a lot of those things, but I've always moved more within the commercial, more competitive side of the industry. I came from commercial music. But I always worked with people who opened my eyes to deep musical worlds. I've been lucky to have with me excellent people with whom I could create the sound I wanted for our music.

Egidio Cuadrado

I have twelve accordions, and each accordion has its songs. I still have the accordion [I used for "La tierra del olvido"]. It's a red Hohner. They're the best. It's very special to me, that accordion. It's one of those old accordions and it's very good. I also recorded many of the songs for *Escalona* with it. There's a section of the song, after the gaita solo, where there's a beautiful accordion part full of harmonized tones. It has a lot of dissonances in the accordion, which are very pretty. I had to practice it a lot. And then my compadre Carlos opens his arms and shouts "AAAHHHHH!" And we have that fusion of gaita, accordion, and guitar.

Iván Benavides

I wasn't thinking of specific harmonies, but afterward I saw the origins. In the accordion, there was a passion for Brazilian accordion. We were a generation that loved Brazilian Tropicália and we wanted to eat up the world and feed from Tropicália, from cumbia, from vallenato, from troubadours.

Carlos Vives

Iván was like a teacher. He had written songs, and in fact, I had performed songs by Iván. Here he was a teacher. "When writing songs, use sonorous words." When I told him the name of the song was "La tierra del olvido," he said, "That's a strong title. It's a phrase for a line in a book. For a movie."

My vallenatos never sounded like a normal vallenato. The way we included the guitars was new. No one had done it like that. But we knew how to do it. We knew the song had a bit of son and cumbia in its DNA. When we got to the studio, we knew how we were going to produce it. We knew we didn't want orchestral arrangements. I knew I didn't want to have that tropical Cuban or Puerto Rican sound. We were establishing a new "tropicality." And since then, a new generation from many regions has understood that and has done what's become a Colombian boon that didn't follow the conventional patterns of tropical music. "La tierra" is a bit of the starting point for that.

Iván Benavides

Almost everything came in one sitting. I took the song to Carlos and then we added the other elements. It didn't have drums. The mood we finally got was very special. And the way we produced was very important because we recorded all the instruments together. We made the demo at the farm. But then we recorded all the instruments [in the studio] at the same time—guitar, bass, gaita—and that generates something very beautiful and something that's been lost since we have Pro Tools. You can hear the individuality in each musician. Nowadays, everything is very produced and you lose that. In this case, since all the songs came from a laboratory [so to speak], in this song Teto is unique. El Papa is unique. As they say in Africa, "I am because we are." That's the overall vibe of the album in general and this song in particular. It was a moment that brings me much happiness and that had such a particular creative group. It generated an aesthetic vision that has allowed Carlos to have a very long career. After that, Carlos and I worked together on noncommercial projects.

Carlos Vives

From the moment I gave it that title, I knew the song would draw attention. Because we all have our forgotten land. It's a cinematic title. I knew it was a brand that would represent us, that defined so much of what was happening with our culture, our territory. With our people forgetting our land and our roots. It's that moment in the life of an artist where you live the moment, you feel the yearning, and you suddenly say, "We have so much here, so much music, why don't we surprise the

industry with something that's ours, but that they can understand? Let's surprise them with something that's not selfish, that
touches them, that feels very modern but has that core strength
that comes from the music."

That's where our head was. That's what the entire team
thought.

It's an album that opens up toward many regions: the Pacific,
the Andes, the plains. I'm going to tell you a story that begins
with "La tierra del olvido," but ends with our world. I'm going
to tell you our real story, including the story of your land. We
wanted to tell the story of a universe that's much bigger than
we think. Colombian music was always seen as very small, but
if you look, you find a universe that's huge, huge, huge. And
Colombian artists are using that universe in many of today's
hits, whether they say so or not.

Iván Benavides

The purists said it was an act of treason against vallenato. But
that treason became tradition. Monsiváis [Mexican writer and
cultural critic Carlos Monsiváis] used to say that tradition is
not the past; it's what will remain in the future. Thirty years
[after "La tierra del olvido"], I feel it's harder to create memorable songs in the twenty-first century. That moment allowed the
creation of songs that unleashed new Colombian music movements. It popularized the gaita, and beyond being a foundation,
these are songs that changed the notion of being Colombian.

Carlos Vives

It wasn't an immediate success. It wasn't going to be that easy after an album like [*Clasicós de*] *La Provincia*. The initial reaction was "Ah, and how many vallenato classics did you record?" None. It was my own song.

It clicked when people felt the nostalgia. The song began to work in different places. Colombian pride opened the doors. That Colombian nostalgia was a motor for our identity and our music. That's what has happened a lot in the United States. People have supported us because of their love and because we rediscovered the power of what's ours, which is marvelous and has touched music all over the world.

Egidio Cuadrado

Yes, it's a very nostalgic song. When we're in concert now, Carlos will dedicate it to Venezuelans. It's a song that always works, no matter where we play it.

Mayte Montero

"La tierra del olvido" says, "I await your return to the land of the forgotten." Which means, I'll wait for you at home. You left, but come back. You have to listen to the entire song to see how it flows and comes together. It's someone who waits for you, like the ocean awaits the river, like land awaits the rain. It's a song that says such beautiful things. As [actress] Amparo Grisales says, it sends shivers down my spine. It's something you cherish. Imagine someone who's far from home and is always yearning for their home, their land, the sounds, everything.

Carlos Vives

It was a before and an after for artists. It was a moment to understand that we could have global hits without losing our local connection. That's what's most important to me. Juanes, Fonseca, many of them recognize it. Many of the artists who sing today use the patterns we discovered at the time.

Nostalgia is the right way to interpret that song. The sadness you feel from being too far away from what's yours. It happened to me. I was singing ballads, I was making soap operas in Puerto Rico, I was doing a lot of things. And filming that *Escalona* soap opera, returning to Santa Marta, to Valledupar, filming in the school my father went to, that was all me. That was mine. I was coming back. But you know what? We can go into the world carrying what's ours. We can be ourselves wherever we are.

I return to drink from this fountain. This is what's mine and this is where I find my sound. I don't need to find it with what someone else does. I can do it with my own elements. That's where all that was born, and that's been our direction.

"Suavemente"
Elvis Crespo
1998

PLAYERS

Elvis Crespo: Singer, songwriter

Jerry Blair: Former executive vice president of Columbia Records / Sony Music

Óscar Llord: Former chairman of Sony Music US Latin

Roberto Cora: Arranger

As the late 1990s rolled around, Latinos were largely absent from mainstream pop culture. Which makes the Latin Explosion that detonated in 1999 all the more remarkable. It would take Ricky Martin's combustive "The Cup of Life" to awaken the world to a Latin way of experiencing music, and his 1999 Grammy performance to get non–Spanish speakers literally off their seats. But as is usually the case with cultural phenomena, the seeds were being sown long before.

With few exceptions, Latin music's global reach has overwhelmingly been tied to up-tempo, danceable music that super-
sedes language and culture.

For literally decades, that realm of "tropical" music, as it was
categorized on the *Billboard* charts, was dominated by salsa,
the successor of the earlier mambo and cha-cha-cha. But in the
1990s, even as salsa continued to thrive and evolve, Dominican
merengue started to creep into the mix. The music, known for its
fast tempo and signature 2/4 beat, was imported into the United
States by the Dominican diaspora, which settled largely in New
York. Merengue, already popular in Puerto Rico by virtue of its
proximity to the Dominican Republic, increasingly began to
mingle with salsa and its purveyors, opening the door to a new
generation of contemporary merengueros with Dominican and
Puerto Rican roots. With its saucy lyrics and easy-to-dance beat,
merengue began to make inroads in the charts, competing head-
to-head with salsa stalwarts. By the mid-1990s, merengue mania
was in full swing. Artists like Olga Tañón, Milly Quezada, and
Proyecto Uno represented vastly different facets of the music
and made it increasingly popular throughout Latin America.
And Sony, along with other major labels, took the lead in promoting the tropical movement. Among the new generation of
acts was Grupo Manía, a merengue version of a boy band. The
group hired Elvis Crespo, a singer with a piercing, nasal voice,
as their front man. It was a short-lived relationship, but it put
Crespo on the map. In 1998, he went solo with the album
Suavemente (*Softly*), whose title track—an infectious, fast-paced
love song set to brash, complex horn arrangements—became
the first merengue track ever to top Billboard's Hot Latin Songs
chart. "Suavemente" spent six weeks at the peak, becoming the
longest-running tropical single ever on the chart (a record that
would eventually be broken by Marc Anthony's "Vivir mi vida"

in 2013). Eventually, it entered the Hot 100, where it peaked at #84, marking the first time merengue ever appeared on that chart.

Most important, "Suavemente" opened the eyes of the record industry to the possibilities of even the most regional of Latin rhythms reaching an international scale.

"This was really the first of the true Latin artists, starting in the Latin market and crossing over into the mainstream market in a big way," remembers Oscar Llord, then chairman of Sony Music US Latin. "It started to open everybody's eyes in the company [Sony] that this was a path."

With multiple remixes and a bilingual version, "Suavemente" became a global hit.

Elvis Crespo

That song was born one day between September and October 1997. I had resigned, or they kicked me out, of Grupo Manía, and, without them knowing I started to record a solo album for Sony. I locked myself up and recorded nine songs, but not "Suavemente." "Suavemente" didn't exist at that time. The album was going to be called *Tu sonrisa* [*Your smile*], for that single. In the process of recording, I realized the company was placing all its efforts on Grupo Manía, and I got depressed, because it felt as if they were just going to shelve me. Banchy [real name Héctor Serrano, the founder of Grupo Manía] very intelligently showed that I wasn't important at that moment. He was very aggressive, and he released an album with a new singer.

Oscar Llord

Elvis was already enjoying success as the key front guy for Grupo Manía. Back at that time, there was also Olga Tañón, Manny Manuel. These artists were already doing 250,000-plus albums in the US Latin market. There was a movement for merengue music. It had that simple 4/4 beat, like disco, and it was easy for everybody in the world to assimilate. A simple beat that's easy to mark. Elvis came to see me very quietly with his manager and expressed interest in going solo.

Obviously, Grupo Manía was at its peak, and letting Elvis take this step could put a damper on the group. As a matter of fact, when we spoke to the Serrano brothers [founders Héctor and Oscar Serrano] they weren't too happy at the possibility of Elvis [going solo]. So, I got a lot of pushback from my own label, especially the guys running the tropical division. I felt the best solution was to let Elvis do the album with his producer Roberto Cora, and after the album was finished, decide if releasing him solo was the right thing to do, or if we should hold him off a little longer.

Roberto Cora

I met Elvis because I was the musical director for Grupo Manía and the owner invited Elvis to be part of the group. At that time, Grupo Manía was recording its second album, which was the first recording I'd done in my life. I was eighteen, nineteen years old. Elvis came to the recording studio when we were already recording. That was my first contact with him. It was very funny because he was coaching a kiddie baseball team, and he came in dressed in his baseball uniform. And then he just comes up and sings his song, top to bottom, in one take. It was like, "Wow! Who is this guy?" It was a very good first impression. We worked together with the group until I left in 1995, when the group was already going strong.

I began working with other artists, and merengue was at its height. Elvis remained with Grupo Manía until the summer of 1997, when he called me and said, "Robert, I left Grupo Manía and I want to make a solo album and I'd like you to produce it." It was a big surprise for me because we hadn't seen each other in all that time. I didn't expect it.

Merengue was very strong at that moment, and there were many recordings happening, many of them featuring a particular sound that was the trademark at the time and that everyone was requesting. If everyone uses the same trumpet player, for example, the sound is going to be similar. But when Elvis and I got together, he told me, "I want to record a solo album, but I need it to be different from the sound that's happening here."

We decided to bring in musicians from the Dominican Republic to record the rhythm. But you never know what life is going to bring. We got hold of Dominican musicians, in this case the guys who played with Hermanos Rosario [a well-known Dominican group], and we booked their plane tickets.

When the day of the trip came, the airline wouldn't let them board with their instruments. They were brass instruments, and because they were so big, they wanted them to check them instead of carrying them on.

They said, "No. If we can't carry our instruments with us, we won't get on." And that was that. They didn't get on [the plane]. We lost the plane tickets. So we started to toss around names of musicians who weren't working on other projects. We had the tambora and the conga, but we didn't have anyone to play the guira. I told Elvis I was playing in a band, and their guira player was pretty good.

He'd never recorded anything in his life, but I thought he

could do it. The three of them got to the studio, and the beautiful thing about all this is, up until then, when I recorded, I would record one instrument at a time. That's how most recordings happen nowadays.

But this time, we decided to record three instruments at the same time: conga, guira, and the tambora. Why am I telling you all this? Because that's where the magic of the album started. When you record three musicians together, they react to one another. And the sound they created . . . we were all looking at each other. That's how we began to record. We did the same thing with the wind instruments. And that's the musical direction we took and that's how the album process began. We knew we had a good, good album. I felt every song in that album could be a single.

Elvis Crespo

I'm depressed, and I go running early in the morning.

When I get back, my son Cuquito is playing PlayStation. I'm all sweaty and I sit down to play with him, but after a while I let go of the controls and I go take a shower. And while I'm under the water, I begin to hum the melody to "Suavemente": "Suavemente, bésame. Que quiero sentir tus labios, besándome otra vez [Softly, kiss me. I want to feel your lips kissing me again]." I sang it again while I showered. And I thought to myself, "This sounds good." I heard the door to the bathroom open, and I figured my son had been in there, but when I looked out from behind the shower curtain, there was no one there. I finished showering, got dressed and went back to playing PlayStation with Cuquito. And he starts, "Suavemente, bésame."

And just like that, Cuquito hummed the melody back at me, perfectly. I said, "Cuquito, where did you get that song from?"

And he said, "I don't know. It just stuck." He was six years old. That's when I realized the melody was special, and I took out my pencil and paper and sat down to write the rest of the lyrics. I began to feel the verses, and the verses just flowed.

Now that I look back at everything and I try to figure out what romantic influence I was getting those days to write that song, I realize that I was watching a soap opera titled *Alguna vez tendremos alas* [*One day we'll have wings*], starring a young Kate del Castillo. That romantic influence, that content, was what was feeding me to write romantic songs. That's where the lyrics to "Suavemente" came from.

I called Roberto Cora and I told him, "Hey, Papo, I have a song." And he tells me, "No, Elvis, man, don't be insecure. You have a great album." Because the album was done. I told him, "No, sir. We're going to record this song." I talked him into it, and we did it.

Roberto Cora

Elvis called me around four, five, six in the afternoon and said, "Robert, this song just came to me. I was taking a shower and I thought of a song that I think is on fire. I think it has something special. I sang it to Cuquito and he kept singing the chorus afterward." He recorded all the lyrics on a cassette tape, and he sent it to me. I got the cassette in the evening, because I like to work early in the mornings. We spoke a little bit about the direction of the song, and then I took it home.

It was one of those few arrangements that simply flow from beginning to end. All the ideas were the original ideas. Each song has its process, and "Suavemente" perhaps was one of those arrangements that were simply open to what came. Almost 90 percent of the final arrangement are things I thought about that same morning. On Thursday, I sent him the demo and he said: "I love it. Let's record it!" We called all the musicians back on Friday, and we recorded the song in one day, like we'd done with the others. Same rhythm scheme, same musicians together. And that's how "Suavemente" was born. In creative terms, those were the three days of chaos.

Elvis Crespo

Roberto brought me an exquisite arrangement. It was a merengue, but it was a wow merengue, with something different, something delicious. It was a contrast. A simple melody with a musical arrangement that demands the trumpets practice to be able to play it. It was a complex arrangement. Roberto Cora brought me a masterpiece. To this day, you hear that arrangement, and it sounds as if it were done yesterday. It's a classic sound.

The song was born with a fast beat: 120 or 118. Those were the beats per minute people were dancing to back then. Now, for example, reggaetón is at 95 or 90. Originally, there was a piano accompanying the voice in the introduction. I decided to leave the intro just with vocals, a capella. It was something I used to do with "La noche [The night]," the Joe Arroyo song I sang with Grupo Manía. I started a capella and people went crazy. Everybody would sing along with me. My tone of voice is one that connects with the masses. It's a strange voice. I felt my voice lent itself to that kind of use. It's a unique voice, a strident voice. And that a capella draws your attention. Same as with "Tu sonrisa."

Plus, I'm a big fan of Celia Cruz with her "Quimbara, cumbara, cumba-quimbambá" [which also starts a capella] and I said, "Let's leave it a capella like Celia Cruz." It was iconic. That introduction is iconic. People listen to it and know that what's coming is special.

Roberto Cora

It's a very particular voice. There are no grays. You like it or you don't. Elvis himself says that he's like a street vendor, hawking stuff in the street. There's no middle ground. You hear the first word that man sings, and you know it's him.

Elvis Crespo

I finish the song, I show it to Sony, and Sony didn't see it. It's shelved because Grupo Manía's album is selling like wow. Like crazy. In fact, the song they had playing on the radio was called "And crazy, and crazy [Y loco, y loco]." They didn't want to make decisions that would bother Banchy, the owner of Grupo Manía. I spent that Christmas, wow, depressed.

Roberto Cora

I had let everyone know that in January I was leaving the group because I was going to get a master's in music in Texas. We turned in the album in August. During the recording process, Elvis had asked me what I thought about the album. At the time, the expectation was that it could sell fifty thousand copies. That was a solid number. That's what comparable groups were doing. So, we turned in the final album, but, obviously, for reasons outside our control, the album wasn't released until the following year.

Oscar Llord

When he finished the album and I heard "Suavemente" in the studio, I felt it was going to be one of those big, breakout records that would create a lot of excitement in the marketplace. So I went back and I told the guys in the label's tropical department that I thought it was best to speak with Grupo Manía and let them know Elvis was going solo. It just became a big scuffle, back and forth. Finally, I got everybody in the conference room and played them "Suavemente," which I felt very strongly about. And I gotta tell you, there was no reaction in the room. People who were there, including my wife, Rosana, will tell you that. I had to play the record over and over—that old thinking that you keep pounding it into people's heads and finally the repetition gets into you. And I set the tone that this would be the lead single.

Elvis Crespo

[Before it was officially released], we began to get the record played in the streets, in the fiestas patronales [patron saint festivities that usually include live music], and the song started to grow organically and to gather steam. The diaspora that came to Puerto Rico to spend Christmas would take the CD back with them to the United States, and DJs in the Northeast started playing it. Oscar Llord noticed that the song started to pop up in the record pools and that's how they decided to release the album on April 14, 1998, and that changed the story. I debuted the album April 11 in Coliseo Roberto Clemente in Puerto Rico.

Oscar Llord

I asked Gabriel Buitrago [currently owner of his own promotion company, Suma], who was doing crossover promotion for Sony Discos, to get some of the DJs to do remixes. He got a guy called Giuseppe D out of New York who did the remix. When we heard it, we loved it. When we first put out "Suavemente," the first reaction was from the Grupo Manía fans, but then it started catching on. When we released the remix, it started playing on Power 96 and caught on fire in clubs all over the country and the crossover process began. To the point that we did over three hundred thousand albums in California alone, a decent tropical market but nowhere near the Northeast or Puerto Rico. And then we went to a million. The first video evolved into the second video. And before you know it, we got him a PR firm, he started doing *The Late Show with David Letterman*, and the record grew. It became a solid #1. It rose to a Top 2 on the dance chart and when I left Sony in 2003, the record in the United States was at 1.3 million copies. No other tropical record had come close. That was a product of the crossover. It expanded his market way beyond his core Latin market. That's the way Elvis emerged. He stepped into a huge platform.

Elvis Crespo

We did a video that I hated back then, and now I love because it's unique. It's a video that transcends time. When the song breaks, there's a Sony convention in Europe and Tommy Mottola [then chairman of Sony Music] wanted to take the song to those countries. But when he saw the video, he said, "Wow, that video is horrible." He sent me to Cartagena with [video director] Simon Brant to film the remix version of "Suavemente." It's a spectacular video, but people like the other one. The one I didn't like.

Jerry Blair

We did an English version, titled "Suavemente, Kissing Me." We worked hand in hand with Oscar to coordinate those efforts. Sony had a third of the market, or more, at the time. You look at what could have mass appeal, and then you talk to your guys in those markets, all the places where you know you could take this stuff and make it bigger. To this day, what shocks me is that the labels still look at it [crossing into other markets] like froth over the cappuccino, but they're not really focused on it. They still haven't figured out how to do it to maximize the opportunity.

Oscar Llord

When Tommy first heard the record, he also thought it was going to be a hit. This was really the first of the true Latin artists, starting in the Latin market and crossing over into the mainstream market in a big way. It started to open everybody's eyes in the company [Sony] that this was a path. And Tommy Mottola, among the global CEOs, was the one who saw it clearest.

"Suavemente" had that simple infectious repetition to it. Elvis was kind of an enigma physically. He had some very unique qualities that made him very singular and distinctive. That, plus the sound of his voice—which is what really distinguished Grupo Manía—plus this incredible remix. Everything. I thought we were going to hit maybe half a million copies, but I never thought it would go to the level of the million-plus. Then it broke in Mexico. I don't recall any merengue record breaking in Mexico before. That's when I knew we had a really big record.

Roberto Cora

I went to the university in Texas in January, and sadly, I never experienced the "Suavemente" boom. They tell me it played at every party. That summer I spent a week in Puerto Rico and I did encounter that craziness of Elvis playing every single day. So much, that I heard his musicians all got together to ask him to please not play so much. To give them a break. We musicians, all we want to do is play, play, play because that's how we make our money.

But in this case, they needed a rest. Crazy.

Elvis Crespo

Did I go into the studio to make a classic song? I went into the studio because something made me happy. It's a song that comes from the soul, full of dreams, and you perceive that.

It's a real song, not forced. And the creative process of the artist with the music was very organic. That's the only explanation I can find. [Just this past year] the song has been in a Huggies [diapers] campaign. It's been in a campaign for the lottery in Israel, with the announcer speaking in Hebrew and the song playing in Spanish. Rihanna danced to "Suavemente" in front of a Christmas tree. Dua Lipa posted, "This song makes me so happy." Artists who weren't even born in 1998 listen to

it. What's most exciting to me is when they told me "Suavemente" was among the tracks NASA astronauts chose to listen
to in their space mission for motivation. That surprised me. My
song was heard in space? That these intellectuals, these geniuses,
would listen to my song to feel happy? I'm blessed. What else
can I ask for, girl? Really. God has been merciful.

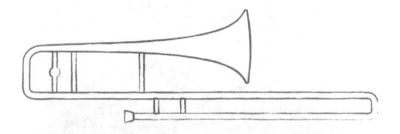

"Smooth"

Carlos Santana & Rob Thomas
1999

PLAYERS

Carlos Santana: Artist

Clive Davis: Former president of Arista Records; current chief creative officer of Sony Music Entertainment

Itaal Shur: Songwriter

Rob Thomas: Artist, songwriter

Back in 1971, guitarist Carlos Santana hit #4 on *Billboard*'s Hot 100 chart with "Black Magic Woman." It would take him nearly three decades to make the Top 10 again, but what a comeback it was. "Smooth," released on June 29, 1999, featuring Rob Thomas on vocals, topped the chart for a stunning twelve weeks and stayed fifty-eight total weeks on the list, making it the #2 Hot 100 song of all time (even post-"Despacito").

"Smooth" was a magical song. Penned by Itaal Shur and Thomas, it was the first single from *Supernatural*, Santana's groundbreaking duets album, which also featured collabs with the likes of Lauryn Hill, Dave Matthews, and Eric Clapton. *Supernatural* hit #1 on the Billboard 200 Albums chart and eventually sold 11.8 million copies in the United States alone, becoming the top-selling album ever by a Hispanic artist, according to Nielsen Music.

It also garnered eight Grammy wins for Santana (tying Michael Jackson's 1983 record for the most Grammys won in a single year), including Record of the Year for "Smooth" and Album of the Year for *Supernatural*. The Song of the Year award, also for "Smooth," was given to Rob Thomas and Itaal Shur as the songwriters, making that the ninth Grammy for the project.

It was extraordinary vindication for Santana, who had never won a Grammy before, and for Clive Davis, the record executive who had originally signed the guitarist back in the 1960s and who took a major gamble with him again thirty years later.

It's tempting to do what some have done and bundle Santana up into the Latin Explosion of 1999. After all, 1999 also saw Ricky Martin's "Livin' la vida loca" and Enrique Iglesias's "Bailamos" hit #1 on the Hot 100. But that wouldn't be accurate. Davis's motivations for re-signing Santana, for committing to the project, had nothing to do with a fad or with a burgeoning Latin movement. It had to do with Santana—the man and the band.

Furthermore, *Supernatural* was never deemed a "Latin" album in the traditional sense of the word, meaning it wasn't predominantly in Spanish, nor did Santana have a tradition of recording predominantly in Spanish. But it was Latin in spirit and direction, built on Latin rhythms and beats, and executed with a global point of view.

"Smooth" might have been sung in English, but what a Latin

homage it was, with its video shot in Spanish Harlem, its multiple visual references (the vintage album covers shown in the opening seconds are priceless for any Latin fan of a certain age), and Rob Thomas's most sincere homage to the music, to the culture, and to his "Spanish Harlem Mona Lisa" (who would become his wife).

Beyond reviving Santana's career, "Smooth" and *Supernatural* were also the big precursors for what is now a standard practice: ingenious collaborations in songs that marry hitmakers from many genres, resulting in expanded listenership. "Smooth" had that in spades: The song played on pop, rock, and alternative radio.

Thanks to the song's long radio run, it also holds a peculiar distinction: "Smooth" ended 1999 as the last #1 song of the decade, and it launched 2000 as the first of the new millennium.

Historic indeed.

Clive Davis

I was with Janis Joplin breaking through, Chicago breaking through, Santana breaking through. I must say the success there was really huge. And it was based on our success and our interaction in those early years that when it came twenty-five years later, and he called me out of the blue and asked me to come see him at Radio City Music Hall [in July 1997], based on nostalgia, affection, all of the above, I did go. At the time, I was with Arista Records, the company I had founded in 1974. It was an unlikely thing, because he was past fifty and he's not a vocalist. But I saw his new band, and I saw that even all those years later, his virtuosity, and the band playing together, it was all there. We agreed to meet. He said, "You know, I went to my spiritual adviser and he asked, 'What do you miss most?' I said,

'I have teenage children and they never hear me on the radio.' I miss not being on the radio. My spiritual adviser asked, 'Who do you associate being on the radio with?'"

And Carlos said he associated it with me. The adviser and his wife at the time, Deborah, suggested that he call me.

So he asked me, "How do you feel about recording me now?" I said, "Look, if we agree to a blueprint, whereby you give me the opportunity to have half the album, to look for natural, organic material that doesn't compromise any of your integrity, I'll do that. The other side of the album will be vintage Santana. You can do with it whatever you want."

Carlos Santana

Clive said something I liked—he was very direct and he used a very spiritual word. "Do you have the willingness? Do you have the willingness to discipline yourself and get in the ring with me, to work together when I start calling everybody in my Rolodex? Will you trust?" He explained that he wasn't into doing just another Santana album—he wanted hits.

Itaal Shur

I was told that Santana was looking for music, so I got a chance to meet with Gerry Griffith [a music consultant who was previously senior vice president of A&R for Arista], who used to work at Arista back in the day. He told me about this opportunity and connected me with Pete Ganbarg [currently president of A&R at Atlantic Records], who was the A&R of the Santana project. And because I got to meet with him, I got to listen to a lot of the songs in the project. A couple of the

songs had the old school Santana. But the collaborations—
none of them seemed to have that original, Santana, montuno
[with a Cuban beat of son montuno] kind of vibe, like "Black
Magic Woman" or "Evil Ways." And I thought, "Okay, I'm just
going to do that." I had the basic groove of "Smooth." I had
a song line that was an outro of a song I had developed with
my band. It was just a starting point. Sometimes you have to
think "What do I have?" instead of starting something new. I
took that and basically wrote a whole song over the weekend. I
used programmed drums, but I added the guitar. The original
demo is me singing a song called "Room 17," about this couple
who are having a hidden affair and rendezvous in room 17.
When I played it for Pete, he liked the music but not the lyrics. They wanted more universal lyrics, and they wanted to
concentrate on love and peace, rather than sexual innuendo or
romantic trysts.

Clive Davis

I later heard that in the company they were calling the [*Supernatural*] project "Davis's Folly." That Davis was being attacked
by nostalgia and affection. How could someone on guitar, over
fifty, who'd never done vocals, break through? But Wyclef [Jean]
delivered "Maria Maria." And then I was working with Lauryn
Hill. Lauryn at the time was writing "A Rose Is Still a Rose" for
Aretha Franklin, and I got her to write a song for Carlos. I read
that Dave Matthews, one of his idols was Carlos Santana, and
that accounted for the fourth of the six tracks I was putting
together for Carlos as the album coproducer. After Pete played
me the track from Itaal Shur, I sent it to [producer] Matt Serletic to play to Rob Thomas. And Rob wrote to it, doing the
demo vocals but never expecting to actually sing on "Smooth."

Rob Thomas

I'd just gotten off the road from our first record [with Matchbox 20]. We were on the road for like three years and I'd moved to New York City. And I got a call from our publisher, Evan Lamberg [then executive vice president at EMI Music Publishing, currently president of Universal Music Publishing Group for North America]. He said, "Itaal Shur's working on a track for Carlos Santana and we want you to come in and help with some lyrics that work." Evan and I had always talked about the idea of . . . Wouldn't it be great if somewhere down the road I'd be working with the band, working solo and writing for other people? And since I had just gotten home, it was just dumb luck. As it turned out, Itaal lived literally two blocks from me. It could have been just that we were close together. And it was really extra nice because they called on Matt Serletic to produce the track.

Itaal Shur

In the end, they took my demo and they just pushed the beat up from 110 to 115 BPM and raised it from A-flat minor to A minor. That took it to the next level. But the arrangement is identical. I have to say, writing it was a very easy thing. There really wasn't any friction making it. It took me a weekend to make the first version; it took Rob Thomas a couple of days to do the lyrics, and then he came to my house and we worked on the chorus. Rob is a great singer. What you hear is how he sounds. And then I heard from the people making the live sessions of the record; it was one or two takes and then overdubs. Nothing was labored. Like a lot of great songs. All the work is getting it to that point.

I grew up with classic rock, and you can't get away from classic rock. But I actually speak Portuguese, my mom was a dancer, and I've always liked Latin music since I was a kid. And then just being in New York City, where salsa is such a part of the culture. I didn't know about Rob and Latin music, but then I met his wife and I got it. He said, "Yes, my wife is Puerto Rican. She's a model." "You just watch her around the house and write about it," I said. "I mean, dude, she's beautiful, she's your muse."

Rob Thomas

There are few people like that, like Santana and Eric Clapton, where the singer is really secondary to the music. I was really aware of the fact that this is something I was doing for Carlos. I was not thinking I was going to sing on it. In fact, I thought George Michael should sing it. But when I got the phrase "Smooth," it was kind of a double meaning. It was about the girl in the song, but it was also about Carlos: "You're so smooth." And so that popped out. I remembered my wife [Marisol, who at the time was Thomas's fiancée] was out somewhere walking around the city. She's half Spanish, half Puerto Rican. And even though she's not from Spanish Harlem, it worked. When I played it for her, I still wasn't sure, and she said, "This is going to be huge." When I met Carlos, the first thing he said was "Hey, you must be married to a Latin woman; that's the kind of thing a white guy married to a Latin woman would say."

Carlos Santana

It sounded like he was in a relationship with a Latina. With all due respect to my Caucasian sisters, he had a different type of sassiness about him. See, we learn to articulate from the females. That's where we get our vocabulary. When a woman puts her hand on her hip and shakes her head, you know she's up to something and has an attitude. That goes into the music. The sassiness is extremely relevant and vital to music; otherwise it sounds bland and ho-hum. I'm not trying to be cute. I'm just saying, real musicians learn a lot from the body language of women. My mom, my four sisters, my two daughters, my wife Cindy. I learned it really quick.

Clive Davis

Rob was so electrifying on "Smooth" as the demo singer that we got Carlos's enthusiasm, and he said, "Let's get that demo singer." Well, the demo singer is the singer of Matchbox 20; it's not going to be that easy to get a release. But through Michael Lipman, Rob Thomas's manager, and with the consent ultimately of Atlantic, we got the OK.

Carlos Santana

When they sent me the demo, it felt a little like an embryonic state. I couldn't tell if it was a boy or a girl [singing], because it looked very embryonic. And by that I mean just the way it looked, soundwise, to me. By that time I was getting antsy pantsy, but it was the last song, we had the album ready, and Clive said, "Please be patient. We need a song like this, and I think it's going to surprise everyone." Clive was always very gentle with his presentation to me, very gracious. And when they sent me the demo, I said, "We need to do it live because right now, I don't believe." For me to believe it, if I'm gonna play the song the rest of my life, I have to feel that it's 150 percent of 100 percent. And Clive pushed the button. We got Matt Serletic and we all decided to do it live. And that's when the energy came in and there's no doubt, not any kind of iota of doubt. As soon as I heard it, even when I was in the middle of the song, I was like, "Man, this song is big." I didn't know it was going to be that big, but I knew it was big. I knew because we'd done that before with songs like "Black Magic Woman." Songs that felt memorable outside of time, and outside of fashion.

Rob Thomas

I flew out to San Francisco and we recorded it together over two days. What's kind of amazing is, the first day I came in the band sussed it out, felt it out. Then what you hear there is three takes. That's a big testament to Matt Serletic and the vision he had when he heard the track. He didn't want it to sound like a dance track; he wanted it to be danceable, but within the Santana context. And Carlos has a signature guitar sound. And then maybe just the moment. For me, I was in the studio with Carlos Santana, and we're in the studio playing together. It was an exciting time and that excitement comes through.

Carlos Santana

It worked by me not even thinking about it. I didn't want it to have brain or mind energy. I wanted it to be with innocence. Innocence es el corazón, the heart. Innocence, to me, is very sacred and very sensual. I think most people—whether atheist or spiritual—people should never lose their innocence. So I didn't practice, purposefully. As soon as I found out where my fingers go on the neck of the guitar, you close your eyes and you complement Rob. Kind of like a minister: He says, "Hallelujah," and you say, "Amen." As a guitar player, when I'm next to Rob Thomas or Rod Stewart, my role is to be present with love and not step on his vocals. Everything I've ever done with [someone like] Plácido Domingo or Rob Thomas—and I mean that in a very soulful way—I know my place. Not like a maître d' or servant. But I am part and parcel of a complete voice. I'm not anybody's shadow and I'm not going to disrupt their light. But I am part of their whole song. I learned that from my dad and from B.B. King. Never compare or compete. That's okay for soccer or for the World Cup. But music is just complementing.

There was a moment, right before the guitar solo, where I knew it was magic. I looked around and I didn't tell anybody, but I could tell by people's eyes that we had found a masterpiece of joy. When you make it memorable, you hang around with eternity. Bob Marley, Michael Jackson, they're memorable. And I don't mean it to sound conceited, but I say it from my heart. I'm thinking, damn, I'm going to be here. I'm going to stay. It's not just music for Americans or Mexicans. It's for humans, period. Twenty years from now you're going to say, "Turn this song up."

Clive Davis

So, look. Did I expect it? Did anybody expect it? I obviously thought we could do nicely or I would not have signed him. But as soon as I played the finished record of "Smooth," Robert Palmese [then Arista's vice president of national promotions], his eyes lit up and he confessed to me, you know, "None of us, no one here ever thought that we would have a commercial record."

Rob Thomas

The record had already been completed and I knew Dave Matthews had a track, and Lauryn Hill, and I felt, this is nice, but maybe "Smooth" will be the pop song. And when they started writing about the record, obviously there were such huge heavy hitters in that record that my name never popped up. And I thought, "Well, this is great, at least I got a chance to work with Carlos Santana, one of my musical idols." I didn't even know it was going to be a single until one day I was walking in SoHo and there was a convertible at the light and these girls were blaring it.

Carlos Santana

I always defer all those things having to do with singles to Clive. I don't even listen to the radio unless it's the [San Antonio] Spurs or something because I'm a Spurs fan. So I know how to trust those who do that all the time. My role is to honor and trust Clive because he is very much consistent with being a support system in my life in a professional and personal way. He and Bill Graham [the concert promoter who supported Santana in his early days] are people that God put on this planet. Because of Clive, there's myself and Whitney Houston; he helped us not only succeed, but he knows when and how to put you center stage. It's impossible to fail.

Clive Davis

How do you break this? How do you bring this to the attention of the Top 40? Yes, he's over fifty. Yes, he doesn't sing. But he's one of the great musicians of all time. We've had a terrific history years ago with the three hits that I mentioned. How do I signal that this is different? I thought, my Grammy party, which had just become a tradition where every major Top 40 player would go. How do I signal that this is different? I had Carlos and Rob Thomas and the Santana band do "Smooth" at my Grammy party, and I also had Wyclef [Jean] perform with the Santana band "Maria Maria." Showcasing those two cuts, they brought down the house with an incredible standing ovation. Word spread immediately from all the tastemakers and power players in that room. And when we went to Top 40 radio, it broke, the album then got nine Grammys—broke the all-time record—and it's a major memory of mine, going up there with Carlos and the album's two coproducers and *Supernatural* becoming among the bestselling albums of all time worldwide.

Rob Thomas

I look at the whole moment like it was a giant parade. It was the *Supernatural* parade, and "Smooth" got to be the first float. You had such a spectacular album. And for me to be kind of an ambassador to that world, and being able to share a totally historic moment, that's really special. Very few people in the world ever get to be a part of something culturally that big. Once we were done with it, there was a lot of talk about let's do something else. And I got called for "The Game of Love" [from the 2002 album *Shaman*], but Carlos and I both felt it just seemed too transparent to come in there and try to re-create that magic again. So I did write some of the songs in the next albums, but Carlos and I have always been kind of precious with what we did with that moment. When I play live, I do a version of it solo that's almost devoid of any guitar because I don't want to re-create Carlos's magic. But whenever we get together, he'll go onstage.

Itaal Shur

I really think this is one of the last all-live bands, sophisticated, mega pop songs in history where there were really class A musicians playing. Quality is something there's not much of anymore. What happened in the 2000s is things started to get more and more programmed. "Smooth" is an anomaly. It could have easily been very corny if you used a drum machine. I feel like I was part of making a worldwide hit that followed the lineage of all great mega pop songs that were made by great musicians like Michael Jackson; people whose talent you could not deny. I feel like "Smooth" was the last megahit of the old music world that was based on talent.

Rob Thomas

I think the song represented a pivotal moment in both of our careers. Carlos in the sense that he'll always be a legend, but there won't be a time when people talk about great guitar players that they don't talk about "Smooth." I think it was great that Carlos had a chance to introduce himself to a new generation of fans. I grew up with "Black Magic Woman" and "Evil Ways," and for kids who grew up now it was "Smooth" and "Maria Maria." But it wasn't like I gave Carlos a career. And it gave me the opportunity to be seen like Rob Thomas the songwriter and not simply the guy from Matchbox 20. It had a huge effect for both of us. Meeting him at the time that I did taught me the difference between being a famous musician and being a celebrity. Not because you're tabloid fodder, but because they like your music. And there's not one birthday or anniversary that I don't get a giant bouquet of white roses from Carlos. White, which means friendship.

Clive Davis

Carlos is a rare human being. He has the best heart, he's bright, he's got ideas—they're abstract, they're spiritual. He aspires at every level of human behavior to be the best. To this day there is no occasion I celebrate regarding myself that is not marked by the most beautiful letter from Carlos, the most beautiful flowers. As I talk to you, my office right now has a huge display of flowers sent by Carlos. He never fails to mention my belief in him from the beginning. It's unique to me in my career. It was not only that I signed him twice. But the huge success we had right from the outset of our careers, and then twenty-five years later to have this all-time success with *Supernatural*. We are bonded. We're always in touch to this day. Our friendship, our relationship, our mutual respect and love, really, I got to tell you, we're not sitting eyeball to eyeball, but we have one of these wonderful, long-lasting, life-nurturing friendships that is very, very special.

Carlos Santana

I'm very grateful to Clive Davis, Itaal Shur, and, of course, Rob Thomas. All three were supremely successful in bringing this masterpiece that makes women very happy.

Quotes from Carlos Santana and Rob Thomas are taken from multiple interviews conducted by the author over a period of years.

"Livin' la vida loca"
Ricky Martin
1999

PLAYERS

Angelo Medina: Former manager

Desmond Child: Producer, songwriter

Draco Rosa: Songwriter

Jerry Blair: Former executive vice president of Columbia Records / Sony Music

Randy Cantor: Arranger

Ricky Martin: Artist

Tommy Mottola: Then chairman of Sony Music; now chairman of Mottola Media Group

February 24, 1999, was just another Grammy Awards ceremony, the performances sedate, the applause polite.

Until a hip-swiveling Ricky Martin cavorted onstage with a fifteen-piece band and a host of dancers and percussionists, who did a conga line up and down Los Angeles's Shrine Auditorium aisle as he sang a bilingual version of "The Cup of Life."

Even before the end of the song, the audience was up on its feet.

With confetti floating down amid the standing ovation, host Rosie O'Donnell faced the camera with something akin to awe on her face.

"I never knew of him before tonight," she said. "But I'm enjoying him soooooo much."

Martin's performance has been called the single biggest game-changing moment for any artist in the history of the Grammys. But it was only the beginning.

"The Cup of Life," with its mix of brash trumpets and Brazilian batucada, was the prelude to 1999's "Livin' la vida loca," the song whose title would come to exemplify an era and a lifestyle.

After his Grammy performance, Martin was again called to the stage, this time to pick up the Grammy for Best Latin Pop Album for *Vuelve*, which included "The Cup of Life."

"Thank you, Robi Rosa," Martin exclaimed, honoring the former Menudo mate who coproduced the album. He also thanked Miami Beach songwriter and coproducer Desmond Child. The gratitude was prescient. Three months later, "Livin' la vida loca," a track written by Rosa and Desmond Child, rose to #1 on the Billboard Hot 100.

The first single off Martin's English-language debut album, it spent a heady five weeks in the top spot and, quite simply, made Ricky Martin the most recognizable music act in the world. Martin's self-titled English-language album would also debut at #1 on the Billboard 200, effectively ushering in what would become known as the "Latin Explosion." A phalanx of other Latin stars followed Martin onto the top echelons of the charts—Shakira, Jennifer Lopez, Marc Anthony, Enrique Iglesias—but Martin was the first.

When Martin performed in 1999, Latin music was not a thing. It was simply not important to the Academy or to the mainstream music industry.

But Tommy Mottola, then chief of Columbia, "had it in his mind that he was going to create this Latin revolution," Grammy producer Ken Ehrlich once told me. At the time, Mottola was already in conversations with several artists, including Marc Anthony, Jennifer Lopez, and, of course, Ricky Martin, to release material in English.

The former Menudo member was a charismatic performer with movie-star looks and moves, and a superstar in the Latin world. He was also bilingual, which at the time was essential to even considering a crossover. Selected to perform the 1998 World Cup anthem, "The Cup of Life," Martin was nominated at the 1999 Grammys for *Vuelve* (*Come back*), an album of mostly romantic material that also included danceable fare.

The Grammys were leery about having a Spanish-language performance—this was prestreaming, of course—but Mottola, who had no doubts about Martin's stardom, pushed hard to have him on the show.

"There was tremendous resistance from the Grammys," Mottola told me some years ago. "They did not want an 'unknown' to perform, yet he had already sold ten million copies of *Vuelve* worldwide. To me, that was absolutely UNACCEPTABLE. No was not an option, and of course the rest was history. Ricky Martin's performance on the Grammys doing 'La copa de la vida' lit the fuse for the Latin Explosion. It took a relatively unknown artist in the Anglo market and propelled him to global superstardom, literally overnight. We followed this [by] immediately releasing 'Livin' la vida loca' and sold over twenty million albums worldwide [of the self-titled *Ricky Martin*]."

Mottola's strategy was key. Had Martin not had an album ready for release following his Grammy performance, had he not had a smash like "Livin' la vida loca" in the wings, the impact may not have been as lasting.

But had it been anyone other than Ricky Martin, the story could also have been much different.

"I gave it all my all," said Martin at the time. "I'm not going to give all the credit to that performance. It was ten to fifteen years of intense work and sacrifices."

And had it been a different time, the effect may have not been the same, either.

The year 1999 was the end of the millennium. There was a sense of hope, of openness. The world was starting to become smaller, the options bigger.

Ricky Martin was on the cover of *Time* magazine's May 24, 1999, issue. The story was titled "Latin Music Pops: We've seen the future. It looks like Ricky Martin. It sings like Marc Anthony. It dances like Jennifer Lopez. Que Bueno!"

While that future eventually waned around 2005, that moment set the stage.

With the right artists and with the right music, a global Latin movement was indeed possible.

And it started with this song.

"Twenty years ago I was extremely fortunate to perform for the first time on the [Grammys] and it undoubtedly became one of the most important and defining moments of my career," Martin told *Billboard* in 2019. "Since then, we have remained focused. Our music has evolved with the times, and there is no denying that Latin music came back to the mainstream charts full force in the last two years, breaking all barriers once again. The world is listening and we are here to stay."

Desmond Child

The year before, I started getting all these reports from different people. My manager Winston Simone's wife, Carleen, had been watching *General Hospital* and was going crazy with this actor/singer called Ricky Martin. Then I got a call from [Miami entrepreneur and promoter] Debbie Ohanian, who said she had seen this kid Ricky Martin and she told [Broadway producer] Richard Jay-Alexander that he should cast him in *Les Misérables*. Richard cast him [in 1996] and started calling me and said this kid was amazing. So finally I called my manager and asked him what the story was. [He] sent me a clip of an aerial view of Buenos Aires where the city was paralyzed because Martin was playing. I think a million people showed up; it was unbelievable. I said, "How can this be?" I was very excited. There was an A&R person at Columbia called Joanna Ifrah, and she was the one in charge of helping develop a crossover album. They arranged a meeting and he came over with Draco Rosa. They'd already had a hit called "María" that Draco [writing under the pseudonym Ian Blake] had cowritten with KC Porter. Ricky lived only six blocks away. He had an entourage of SUVs, and they came in and Draco was very quiet, holding a Bible that he was reading in the corner. We bonded. All of us. And so we started.

The first song we actually wrote together, Draco and I, was "The Cup of Life," on the plane from Los Angeles to Miami. This was amazing. It was 1998. Thank God France won [the World Cup], and with them winning, the song just took off and it was #1 in twenty-three countries simultaneously, apparently overnight. Because it became such a big hit, this song was also included at the last minute on an album that he was just finishing called *Vuelve*.

Jerry Blair

Deborah Castillero was my ex-wife. I knew what was going on in the Latin market because of her. So I convinced Tommy Mottola to make her our Latin consultant. She said, "There are two acts you need to focus on first: Shakira and Ricky Martin." We saw then that this was essentially urban music and whoever liked urban music was going to like this. It's universal. Ricky was signed to Sony International and it was a matter of what label he was going to be on. He signed to Columbia. We released "María," then we did a remix, and then we recorded the bilingual version of "María." That was the beginning that sparked Ricky.

Tommy Mottola

With "La vida loca," a lot of that happened with a guy named Jerry Blair. His ex-wife was so invested in Ricky and Latin music before anybody else. And Jerry was in my ear constantly and I green-lit the whole thing because I just thought, "If this guy [Ricky Martin] could ever perform in English the way he performs in Spanish, this would be the greatest global phenomenon."

Angelo Medina

Ricky and I were looking for the American Dream, and we were looking for an original sound. At that point, we had made albums that were more "normal." In the crossover process, we recorded "The Cup of Life," which was fantastic. And two things came together: Draco, who wanted to be an alternative artist and wanted to do art, and Desmond Child.

Tommy Mottola

He had just come out of the World Cup with "La copa de la vida," and we were releasing the album shortly after that. I remember calling Mike Greene, who ran the Grammys at the time. He rejected putting Ricky on [the show]. I got extremely disturbed about that. We had some words about it. And I said to him, "Perhaps Sony shouldn't be involved in the Grammys this year if you feel so strongly about it, because we believe this is going to be one of the highlights of the show, and one of the biggest events ever in the history of the Grammys and the world musically." And he completely disagreed. [Grammy producer] Ken Ehrlich, everyone else was on board. All those guys were 100 percent on board. But Mike Greene was the dictator at the time and they were all pretty afraid of him. I think at that time I went over his head to Les Moonves, who was running CBS, and convinced Les that this was a great move. Long story short, we put enough pressure on him that we got a huge slot for Ricky. And the rest is history. Simple as that. Madonna was sitting in the front row. You could see her jump up. I'm sitting in the audience. This is like watching fucking Elvis Presley for the first time when you saw him on *Ed Sullivan*. It really was. It was groundbreaking. And he didn't even do "Livin' la vida loca." The performance was undeniable. And then we released "Livin' la vida loca."

I was 100 percent aware that we were making history. Not because I'm a genius, but because it was undeniable. You looked at it, and you knew and you saw the making of a star. A star was born, who was already a star. A huge star. But this was ground-breaking for him.

Desmond Child

Then I started working on other songs for the English album, like "Private Emotion." And right toward the end, Angelo [Medina] called me and, because of the success of "La copa de la vida" at the Grammys, he says, "We need a song that's in Spanglish. We need something to follow up this performance." At that moment Angelo was desperately trying to get everybody who was writing and producing this album to wrap it up and turn their tracks in for mastering because we had to get it out fast. Ricky had to be the first one.

Sinatra had passed away the year before and there was a lot of this Rat Pack music that was being played and all these retrospectives and we had that in our system. We thought Ricky is like James Bond meets Elvis. Let's make him the Latin Elvis. We created this song that was meant to be sort of Elvis-y, but also had that Rat Pack Sinatra thing. "She's into superstitions," "The Lady Is a Tramp" kind of thing. It had swing.

The thing is, it had to be in Spanglish. We spent like three days driving each other crazy. Draco was working with our arranger, Randy Cantor, in one room, and in the other I was trying to figure out the storyline and the lyrics that fit the story; the Latin James Bond/Elvis story.

Woke up in New York City in a funky cheap hotel
She took my heart and she took my money
She must've slipped me a sleeping pill

I had a lot of trouble with the idea of what was Spanglish. It had to be words that if you were an English speaker you actually knew what it means in Spanish. I started thinking, "What does everybody know? El Pollo Loco. There's a Pollo Loco everywhere. Who doesn't know that?" And that's when I said, "Livin' la vida loca." *Livin'* was a lucky word for me because I had cowritten "Livin' on a Prayer." That was my lucky word, so I threw it in there.

Draco Rosa

There were a few songs that were written on a plane. A lot of these things, at least the birth of it, was flying in the skies together and writing on a plane with Desmond. [For "Livin' la vida loca"] I'm a big fan of the Doors. For that chorus— "Upside, inside out"—I had [Jim] Morrison in my head. I had the Doors. I had that in my head, energetically. I always love that because it reminds me of my own childhood. At one point, after putting the demo together, Desmond said, "Wow, it's awesome, but we have to clean this up a little bit more for Ricky, because it's a little bit heavier and more intense." It's nice to work with Des because he has that touch. Pa' que le llegue a más gente [Bringing it to more people]. So it's nice to have that yin and yang of working with him. He has that other side to my free spirit and it's pretty cool.

When we were [writing] in Miami at his desk, we just sat there with notepad and guitar. Desmond is the songwriter's songwriter. I'm so in the moment I don't recall a lot of these things. I just recall the Morrison story. When I was laying down that chorus and feeling with the melody line, I couldn't stop thinking about the Doors. It was a production thing, energetically. It was a little bit more aggressive. Especially back then, I was a little bit more melancholy.

Angelo Medina

My secret weapon was Draco, who didn't want to do that song because he didn't want to do anything Menudo-related. He got together with Desmond, and [as they say in Spanish], hunger and a desire to eat got together. Then Luis Gómez Escolar redid some things in the Spanish lyrics, but Desmond and Draco were essential.

Desmond Child

I delivered the demos to the record company and someone said, "The song's terrific, but can you write it in English now?" And I said, "It is in English." And he said, "It sounds like it's in Spanish. You have to write in English—no one knows what 'vida loca' is." At one point they ran a full-page ad in *Billboard* that said LIVIN' LA VIDA LOCA, and underneath, it said, LIVIN' THE CRAZY LIFE. We did a Spanish version with Luis Gómez Escolar. We had worked with him before on "The Cup of Life." He did the Spanish translation of that. "Como Caín y Abel, es un partido cruel [Like Cain and Abel, it's a cruel game]." Those were his fantastic lyrics. The arrangement? We worked it out together with our arranger, Randy Cantor, who actually ended up getting a Grammy nomination.

Guitars? Draco did that overdub with Paul McCartney's guitarist, Rusty Anderson . . . he wanted to get that surfer sound. It was a kind of mélange, a composite of impressions. Because we were going for that kind of '60s retro sound.

Randy Cantor

Desmond flew me down to Miami because he wanted me to work on Ricky Martin stuff. Ricky was my first Latin pop album. I knew who Ricky was because I sort of knew who Menudo was. I knew "The Cup of Life." I did work for Desmond before, but I hadn't been in Miami before.

[For "Livin' la vida loca"], Desmond and Robi Rosa had a loop going, and a melody that kept repeating over and over again. It was sort of like a carnival. Like a marching band doing something in Rio.

Desmond had a really big place on the bay on Pinetree Drive and I was staying at a guesthouse. I'm from Philadelphia. I listen to all kinds of music, but I speak a very, very small amount of español. That wasn't my foundation. My foundation was rock 'n' roll and R&B. But they basically said, "Here's the loop and the melody and made a few suggestions." He wanted that kind of sound because the World Cup song also had that kind of bombastic feel. They basically gave me carte blanche to come up with whatever I wanted to do.

The way Desmond works, he'll leave me for two or three days and then he'll come back and say, "No, no." Or "I like that part, I like that part." Until it became what it became.

[Draco] is a fucking brilliant guy. I was messing with the surf guitar and he loves surf guitar. And Desmond is a genius. He knows what he wants. He wanted it to rock like a rock song, but not lose its Latino element. It had to be exciting. I met Ricky and I watched his dancing. I immersed myself in it. But just being around Miami. Going to Lincoln Road. Meeting people. It just worked. I stumbled into things like Inspector Clouseau.

Desmond Child

I had developed one of the first Pro Tools studios [Pro Tools is the digital audio software that is now the standard for music production, and includes thousands of instruments and sounds].

And "Vida loca" was done all with computers and in the box, as they called it. It was the first song totally recorded and mixed in the box that went to #1. It was 100 percent digital. Prior to this song, most Latin music in Miami was done in very beautiful studios with very special reverb. We didn't have that. And when you hear it on the radio, because it's dry, it's not swimming in an echo, it gets in your face. At that point, I listened to a lot of urban music, and it was very dry and sounded like it was all done in Pro Tools. We didn't know this, but we made sound recording history with that record.

It was all done in my converted garage, which I named the Gentleman's Club. One of the things about it is this: I wanted to bring to it what I had learned writing stadium anthems—the kind of fist-high-in-the-air element—to Latin music. So "The Cup of Life" goes, "Here. We. Go. Ales, ales, ales." "Vida loca" was a little more sophisticated with the syncopated "Up. Side. In. Side. Out." More like a Fosse dance routine gone arena rock.

I wanted it to be cinematic, so what is being sung by the lyric is being supported by the music like a movie score. For example, the start of the second verse ends with a gong: "Woke up in New York City." It's Chinatown.

Randy Cantor

It almost has a reggae element to it, too. Like there was a guitar on the upbeat, like a reggae song. But it started as an organic loop of a marching band in Brazil. Ricky loved that kind of music, and "The Cup of Life" was of that flavor, too.

To create that gong, I put a smash cymbal kind of noise. Desmond said, "I want it to sound like a huge explosion." "Woke up in New York City," and I hit a whole bunch of keys.

Desmond Child

We sent the demo to Ricky, and Draco put the guide vocals on the demo. Ricky learned the song while he was touring. Angelo had him touring night and day. We'd get him for a sliver of time, and then he had to run to Crescent Moon to sing some of Emilio's songs [Emilio Estefan was also producing songs for the album]. He was ping-ponging. The vocal booth was the corner of the garage. At one point I said, "Okay, you cannot leave the vocal booth."

He said, "I need to go to the bathroom." Alice Cooper had told me how producer Bob Ezrin used to chain him to a chair or duct-tape him to a wall to get him to sing "Welcome to My Nightmare." So, as a joke, I said, "No, you're not allowed to go to the bathroom. You cannot leave that room until you sing that song." I told him he could pee in one of his water bottles and he did, just to prove that he could be a good sport. It was a big joke. But it worked. He had so many responsibilities: He was doing interviews in the middle of takes.

It needed like two hours with him really concentrating. He had a wonderful guide with Draco's vocal, because Draco has that kind of laid-back thing [when he sings], and those drops in his voice—"Uup" [mimics the sound of the vocals dropping]. That's what gives the song the swing. A lot of Latin music at that time was sung by crooners who had a lot of vibrato. I forbade vibrato. No vibrato. Just sing it and do the dive down at the end of the phrases.

Ricky Martin

Even the recording process was magical. For "Livin' la vida loca," I was lucky to work with Draco Rosa and Desmond Child. Although I'd done many albums, I quickly realized that working with Desmond was another level. Desmond is a musical giant: He's sold 300 million copies, has worked with Aerosmith, Bon Jovi, Cher, all the big ones.

Desmond Child

When it was time to make the video, Draco and I explained the song to Ricky this way: "Elvis in Vegas. All black." We watched footage of Elvis in Vegas. That was a huge influence. People in front were choreographed, rather than just a random crowd. So it had a very theatrical vibe. I think together we accomplished our vision. We saw Ricky as the Latin James Bond Elvis, and then he put his magic, and his own creativity, his look, and he took it to a level beyond anything we could ever imagine.

Ricky Martin*

"La vida loca" is amazing. It's amazing to play with the sounds of the '60s, with ska, with a little bit of that classic guitar

---

* "Ricky Martin Interview – 1999," YouTube video, 06:31, "Lachlan Hyde," May 11, 2014, https://www.youtube.com/watch?v=Si37ihIPw0w. Ricky Martin declined to be interviewed for this book.

sound. And you have to create this character: Livin' la vida loca, baby. It's not you anymore. It's this guy having this day with this crazy woman who's driving him crazy. It happens to every one of us.

Desmond Child

When you're working with a real star, you can do that. I think one of the things my mentor Bob Crewe always said was that a star is not just one star. Up in the sky it looks like a huge single star, but it could be ten stars aligned that gives it that strength. There's the star, the performer, then the song, the production, the management, the PR, the promotion. It takes all those things to align, and it takes a person who doesn't crumble under pressure. Because Ricky was a child star, he knew the discipline and his role. He's so polite and loving to everybody. I've never seen him cross.

Ricky Martin*

People often ask me why I think "Livin' la vida loca" was so successful. On the one hand, I think the world at that moment was ready to hear something new. But more than that, on my end, all the pieces were in place. At the time I had a great manager, a great record label, a great production team, and we were all in sync and had the same mantra of winning and going above and beyond. Aside from that, I had a great album in my hands. In the end, that's the most important thing of all: the music. The music can cross and break barriers between people and cultures.

---

*   Ricky Martin, *Me* (New York: Penguin Group, 2010).

Jerry Blair

It was laying the foundation. I remember being down at Desmond's house, and we knew these songs were going to be smashes. I remember the videos. And we got the car from the video, and he pulled up in it on Sunset Boulevard for the record signing. Ricky opened the door. After Ricky, after the success of "Livin' la vida loca," we approached it where we attacked that marketplace in a more pronounced way, as opposed to being limited in scope. With Ricky, the word *crossover* was a poisonous word for me. What we did was broaden the audience.

Randy Cantor

When they finished it, it was really good, but I never imagined it was going to be the biggest thing. Right after I did it, I went skiing. And a friend of mine said, "Did you work on that Ricky Martin track? It's going to be the biggest record that ever was." I got back and it was Ricky-mania. But Ricky Martin is undeniable. First of all, he's probably the nicest human being I've met in my life. He is so righteous, so genuine, and so real.

Draco Rosa

When I think of the song now, I love it. I get so excited. I go wow. As a chamaquito [little boy], people would say, "Oh there's always a Beatles song playing somewhere in the world at any given second." It's mind-blowing. And "La vida loca" is a song so many have heard, you know? It's an achievement. It's a great feather in my cap. One of the prettiest ones. I'm super proud. I love Ricky. That moment in my life is extremely important. It opened the doors to so many things. I got a recording studio. That song changed my life. This is a songwriter's jewel. So I'm very blessed, very humbled. I'm the last one in that line, but here in the line.

Desmond Child

We knew it would be a success from the beginning. The title dictated the whole journey. For the song to become a Hot 100 #1 was a true satisfaction for us, a job well done. I have produced twenty-seven songs for Ricky Martin, but "Livin' la vida loca" changed the course of popular Latin music forever. It was the fuse that ignited the Latin music explosion.

Ricky's "Cup of Life" performance [at the Latin Grammys] definitely lit the first match, but followed by "Livin' la vida loca," it was a one-two punch.

Tommy Mottola

We were starting something that became a movement and is now the global music of the world. And we created the Latin Explosion. Every one of my artists ended up on the cover of *Time* magazine. And that made me so proud, to feel I was a part of that and I had my hand in that. For me, it was critically important for our company to be the leader in a multicultural, global sound of artists from the Latin region, who I was personally connected with, musically connected with, and emotionally connected with.

"Whenever, Wherever"
Shakira
2001

PLAYERS

Emilio Estefan: Producer, manager

Shakira: Artist, songwriter

Tim Mitchell: Artist, songwriter, producer

Tommy Mottola: Then chairman of Sony Music; now chairman of Mottola Media Group

Ricky Martin's phenomenal success opened the door for a string of Latin artists who waved the flags of their heritage, but who sang in English. The hits started coming out so quickly that the media and the industry coined the term *crossover*, created to identify those acts who began their careers in Spanish but could "cross over" into the English and global markets. As Martin continued to top the *Billboard* charts, Sony Music Chairman

Tommy Mottola was readying releases by Marc Anthony and Jennifer Lopez, both born and raised in the Bronx to Puerto Rican parents. But then he decided to take on an even bigger challenge. Why not release an English-language album by a Latin American artist? Mottola zeroed in on Shakira, the young Colombian star who was redefining the parameters of women in rock. Shakira already had multiple global hits under her belt, a multiplatinum-selling album (*¿Dónde están los ladrones?* [*Where are the thieves?*]), and a famous manager, Emilio Estefan, widely regarded as the most influential Latin music executive at the time. But not only was Shakira not from the United States, she didn't speak English. Breaking her into the mainstream market seemed like a monumental task.

"Without question it was a challenge," says Mottola. "I thought a breakthrough like this would be huge. Absolutely huge."

An album was set in motion. Estefan and his wife, Gloria, who was close to Shakira and served as one of her mentors, encouraged her to write and sing in English. Gloria also stepped in to translate "Suerte" (which directly translates to "Luck") into "Whenever, Wherever," one of only a couple of songs on the album originally written in Spanish.

Once *Laundry Service* was completed, Mottola, as company chairman, made a decision. Shakira's first English-language single would be "Whenever, Wherever."

The song, aided by a Spanish version that was marketed to Latin audiences and a video that highlighted Shakira the dancer and showed her diving off a cliff, became her first charting title on the Hot 100 chart, peaking at #6 on the December 29, 2001, chart.

It would become her second-longest charting title on the chart, staying for a total of twenty-four weeks ("Hips Don't Lie" and "La tortura [The torture]" both charted for thirty-one weeks), and it would effectively break Shakira into the mainstream market, making her an international star.

Nearly twenty years later, the appeal of "Whenever, Wherever" hasn't subsided. The song was part of Shakira's Super Bowl performance on February 2, 2020. The following week, the song debuted at #54 on *Billboard*'s Digital Song Sales ranking, while *Laundry Service* reentered the Billboard 200.

Tommy Mottola

Shakira had been signed to our Colombian company since she was fourteen years old. I had followed her career way back with her Spanish albums, and we had released *¿Dónde están los ladrones?* and had huge success. I remember first meeting with her like a year and a half before [the album release in 2001], telling her it would be a big step if she was able to do an album in English. She said, "I don't know if I can do it, but I think I can."

Shakira

I do think there was great anxiety surrounding the crossover. A part of me was definitely more anxious than I thought I was. But it was also something I'd waited for a long time. A dream was coming true. A longtime dream. The court was opening up, my field of play was expanding, and that didn't come alone. It came with great challenges, like learning how to speak English properly, and giving a decent English interview.

Tim Mitchell

I started working with Shakira in 1998 as sort of her musical director and playing guitar during the promotion of her *¿Dónde están los ladrones?* album. After that, we did the *MTV Unplugged* album together, and then we jumped into *Laundry Service*, which was this whole next level of things. At the time, Emilio Estefan was also managing me as a producer, and I'd been playing guitar with Gloria since 1991 with the Miami Sound Machine. But when I met Shakira, I didn't know who she was because I was kind of a gringo who grew up in Detroit. But we just kind of hit it off from the very beginning. All the music she liked was all the stuff that I was into: a lot of rock 'n' roll, a lot of progressive, alternative music, and all this stuff. So we started writing together after rehearsals and just hanging out, and when it came time to write her English album, it was just more writing. We spent many weeks and months just writing. I went to the Bahamas a bunch of times and we went to Uruguay and wrote down there in Punta del Este, and there were a lot of people involved in the writing process of the album.

Shakira

I really wanted to do a song that brought together Andean sounds. I've always loved Andean music, the sound of the bombo leguero [a traditional Argentine drum], Andean flutes. I've always connected with that music, and I wanted to do some pop, something popular, but that also had that tint. I was clear in that I wanted to play with those ideas.

Tim Mitchell

I was always thinking of trying to write her a song like Natalie Imbruglia's "Torn," but that song was a very major harmony song. I was in Crescent Moon [Estefan's studio in Miami] the day before I went back to the Bahamas to work with her, and I was thinking, "I need to find a way to do this [in a minor key]." I wanted to do like a four-on-the-floor kind of thing, and I came up with a kind of a minor chord version of what I thought was similar to what I was going after. In the Bahamas we had a nice little writing room at this house. It was awesome, and I just programmed a beat, drums, and these chords, and then once Shakira gets involved, everything is super creative. She had this idea for an Andean flute kind of thing and she pretty much sang it to me. At the time we were really into guitars, and she was into guitars and rock, so I tried to do like a Hendrix-y sort of rhythm part, and then that kind of became the guitar part. And then the intro part, there's this guitar line [sings intro bars of "Whenever"]—I came up with that. I was thinking of it like a James Bond kind of thing.

I didn't have any melody coming in. I just had the chords and the groove, and the idea. Then we got in the studio together, started riffing back and forth. She's amazing with melodies. All the melodies, like [sings melody of "Whenever"], that's all her for sure. I can't stop her. She's brilliant with melodies and stuff.

Tommy Mottola

She has her own perspective and point of view, hands down. She knew exactly what she wanted this to sound like. And what I loved is, it had the flavor of the Andes, but yet, with all those sounds—the flute and the percussion—it had this international pop/rock sound and feel. And that came from her. That absolutely came from her.

Shakira

I have a vague memory of having recorded a flutist we brought from Argentina. But it was a whole process to get the best out of him. I remember I dictated the melody, which is something I also do a lot. When I have the arrangements, I imagine the melodies the instruments play and I dictate them to the musicians. In this case, it was hard to dictate what I wanted. Because folk musicians have their own way of doing things. I would say, "No, no, no, not like that [she sings a beat]." The guy would suddenly take a different turn. I was very clear on the melody I wanted and what I wanted the flute to do.

Tim Mitchell

We brought the Andean flute player from Argentina. I already had [the flute part] programmed, so we layered what he did with what was there already just to keep things tight. The song ends with the flute. I programmed all the percussion ideas, and then I just redid everything with live percussion. A lot of the percussion that's happening are loops, but for the buildups I had orchestra drums, big kettledrums. The intro to the song, where you hear this swell into the downbeat, that was actually this giant orchestra drum. Just one hit, and then I reversed it and swelled it, so that's the swell into the downbeat of the song after the guitar intro. I used lot of little tricks back then, but all in all it was super fun. I still love the song, so that's always a good sign—if you love one of the songs that you wrote, and the way it was produced.

Emilio Estefan

She also wanted him to play the drums, because she wanted something more typically Argentine. But he couldn't get on the right beat. They finally used him on the flute, but not the drums. In the end, I played. And Tim, who was my coproducer [on the album], said, "Don't worry about it, Emilio. I love the feel. It's combining Miami Sound with Latin America." With Shakira you had to make a fusion that was international.

Shakira

I remember leaving Crescent Moon, [Emilio Estefan's] studio in Miami. We had recorded part of the instrumentation, but we didn't have the chorus. I was driving down US 1 and it was like two in the morning. I used to work late at night before and I'd drive at those hours. And while I drove, I came up with the chorus, and I started to sing, "Contigo, mi vida, quiero vivir la vida. Y lo que me queda de vida, quiero vivir contigo." I was so excited, I started to shout, alone in that car. Because I thought, "This is a bomb." When I get that feeling, when that happens to me, I don't have the slightest doubt that the song will do well with listeners and will become a hit. That doesn't always happen. But that was one of those moments where I felt that certainty. I thought of everything—melody, chorus, and lyrics—simultaneously. That's not common, either. Sometimes you write the words first, or you think of the melody and you search for the words that fit the melody. But it happened just as I'm telling you. Contigo, mi vida, quiero vivir la vida. Y lo que me queda de vida quiero vivir contigo. It was question-answer, immediately, with words and melody, and I started to shout like a crazy person all alone.

Tim Mitchell

Gloria [Estefan] came up with the lyrics for the English hook. She basically did a translation of the Spanish lyrics into English. Then Shak and I got together, and Shak wanted to keep certain things the same. Like she had that line: "Lucky that my breasts are small and humble, so you don't confuse them with mountains." I was literally like, "Are you sure you want to do that?" Thank God I didn't talk her out of it, because it's such an interesting lyric. I had to bite my tongue. So, learning experience there, for sure.

Shakira

Well, it was creative license. It was a love song. It was a song that had a muse. I wrote it for my ex, who was my significant other at the time. That was the purpose of the song. That's why it talks about distance and crossing the Andes to see him, because he lived in Argentina at the time. I was madly in love. My lyrics have always been very autobiographical and colloquial. That's how I really felt. Well, how I still feel because, as a matter of fact, my breasts still remain small and humble even after two kids, and I gotta say, they look intact. It's a miracle. It's a true miracle.

Tommy Mottola

The fact that she was just learning how to speak English was actually an advantage for her. It was more like poetry. She was expressing herself in a way that was lyrically out of the norm—those are the best words I can use to describe it. It was more expressive and more poetic than a normal, straightforward lyric. I was stunned and shocked at the way she made references to things. I thought it was absolutely brilliant.

Shakira

We recorded in Spanish first. At the time, my English was pretty precarious, so I asked Gloria Estefan to help me with the words. And she did a pretty faithful adaptation of the Spanish lyrics. That was the kind of push I needed to jump into the water and begin to swim on my own. I think that was the only song I needed someone to do an adaptation for. From that moment on, I began to work with a Spanish-English dictionary. I also had a blue thesaurus that [producer and composer] Luis Fernando Ochoa gave me. He said: "Shaki, this is going to be really helpful. This is going to help you tremendously [speaks with a Bogotá accent]." I had no idea what a thesaurus was. "Here you have every synonym and antonym. This is what you'll need for the rest of your life." I started to navigate the famous [Roget's] thesaurus. And I started to write songs. I remember the next song I did, the first one I wrote by myself in English, was "Objection." And I'm telling you, I wrote it with pretty precarious conversational English skills. But from that moment on, things changed for me.

Tim Mitchell

It was originally written in Spanish. It was called "Suerte," and she had great lyrics and was inspired by her current situation and all this stuff; it was fantastic. It wasn't until later that the idea came up to do it in English. It was never supposed to be the first single. It was one of these songs that came up in the background, that kind of bubbles up to the surface.

And then it's funny because, as it went along, I started programming a lot of drums and percussion, and a way to catapult this into the chorus, and it just came out so well. I think it's one of those things that, because we didn't put so much pressure on it, because it was never slated like "This is the first single, so it has to be perfect," it worked better.

Shakira

Tommy Mottola decided it should be the first single. I have to give credit to him because I thought it was going to be "Objection." We were between "Objection," "Whenever, Wherever," and "Underneath Your Clothes." He said, "It has to be 'Whenever.'" It was his initiative completely. I had doubts. But he was so sure that was the first single. And he was right.

Tommy Mottola

I was part of the process the whole time it was going on because we were dealing with it in Miami and several other places where she was at the time. I heard a couple of things along the way and then she came in and she played me the whole album. And I thought we were going to have one of the biggest hits I'd ever heard. She came to New York to see me in my office, one on one, shut the door, and sat across from me at my desk with a yellow legal pad, going over every detail of her notes. She always came with a yellow pad; she had notes and she took notes. She's very methodical when it comes to that stuff. She's an extremely detailed, highly intelligent, and opinionated woman. I loved it. I loved how much she was engaged, and I loved engaging with her. We went through every song and I told her what I thought the singles were. She wanted "Objection." I said, "This is a mistake. I think you're wrong. I think ['Whenever, Wherever'] is a #1 record." She disagreed. It just happened that shortly after I met with her, I saw the head of Z100 and I played it for him. I remember him saying to me, "Can I have this tonight? This is a #1 record. We'll blow it up." And that was the end of the story.

Emilio Estefan

She wasn't sold on the song. But Sony's feedback was "That's the song." I laugh because, years later, I saw her in a Pepsi commercial and the song they used is "Whenever, Wherever."

We created a unique sound, a sound that was her. Shakira is about fusion. It's not forced; it's something she carries in her. She wanted to make sure her sound was different. I told her, "This sound is mid-tempo and it will be global."

Tim Mitchell

I was shopping for some gym shorts at that Sports Authority in South Miami, and she called me, and was like "That's the first single, mister." I was like "Holy shit, the first single? Wow, amazing!" You cannot hope for anything better than having the first single. I'll never forget that comment. I don't know if she remembers, but I remember that moment for sure. Because you never know what's gonna happen, you know? You can release the first single, and nothing happens. So I was super excited, but at the same time trying to be realistic.

Shakira

The video was my introduction to society. It was very important that it look genuine and that in some way it reflected who I was artistically. An essential part was for me to look very organic, very earth, very air, very water, very fire. Elemental. Primary. I had to be barefoot, with my hair down, moving in the way I know to move, which isn't taught, which is the way I feel music. And that's what we got. I've always felt that way. I'm not a very polished artist. I don't think I'm a very polished artist. Somehow I feel I'm still raw, even after all these years. I don't know if that's a good thing. I didn't want to change my personality or tell a story that wasn't true. I think it was my first video with a great director, Francis Lawrence, who a short time later started making films in Hollywood.

Tim Mitchell

I loved the video. This was the introduction of this girl, and her persona came out, in my opinion, very different from what was happening. She's a great dancer, she does all these things, but she also incorporated this sort of super-artistic, international vibe. It wasn't just like a Miss Latin artist who dances, and da da da. I thought the video reflected the song, and it reflected her. [The song] did so well. It went #1 all over the world. We promoted it for like a year, obviously pre–social media. Now you don't even have to leave your bedroom to promote an album, but at the time, it was a whirlwind. We were doing a sound check for some TV show a few years ago, and they were playing "Whenever, Wherever" in the background over the PA. And she turns to me and says, "How did we do that?" The fact that it just flowed so easily, she sang it great, there was no pressure put on that song, and that had so much to do with it just flowing. We didn't overthink it, and now I overthink everything, so [laughs]. But I try not to.

Shakira

I got sick before doing *The Rosie O'Donnell Show*. I got so sick. All my defenses went down because I was terrified of American television. I think I still am. It was the live factor. I'd never done live television. In Latin America, everything is prerecorded. Now, not only did I have to do it live, but in English. The *Rosie O'Donnell* appearance provoked a ton of anxiety. I think it was my first interview on American television. But none of that came alone. It came with huge fears, expectations, adrenaline, and desires, and all those emotions that weren't easy to digest for a twentysomething girl. It's still not easy to digest at forty-three. It's a song that comes full of so much emotion. A song that's given me great happiness and has been the bridge to so many other places in the world. I have a lot to be grateful to it for.

"Gasolina"

Daddy Yankee
2004

PLAYERS

Carlos Pérez: Owner of Elastic People; video director and creative director

Francisco Saldaña (Luny): Producer

Gustavo López: CEO of Saban Music Group; then president and founder of Machete

Daddy Yankee (Raymond Ayala): Artist, songwriter

In mid-July 2004, an album titled *Barrio fino* (*Elegant neighborhood*) seemingly jumped out of nowhere into the #1 spot on the Billboard Top Latin Albums chart.

The artist was Daddy Yankee—real name: Raymond Ayala—a Puerto Rican reggaetonero little known outside the island at a time when reggaetón was just beginning to encounter commercial success. But in Puerto Rico, Daddy Yankee was king, the leader of a new musical movement born in the barrios and connecting with hundreds of thousands of fans who identified with a message created in their own streets.

Barrio fino's success was duly noted by the industry; after all, it was the first reggaetón album to debut at #1 on the chart. Moreover, Yankee was an independent act, signed to his own label, although distributed by UMVD via a deal with another indie, VI records.

But then came the song.

"Gasolina," the first single off *Barrio fino*, was written by Yankee with his frequent collaborator, Eddie Dee, and produced by Luny Tunes, the visionary production duo made up of Francisco Saldaña (Luny) and Victor Cabrera (Tunes) who continue to produce some of the top-performing artists and tracks in urban music. The song never rose past #17 on Billboard's Hot Latin Songs chart because so few Spanish-language stations played urban music at the time. Instead, helped by remixes with Lil Jon and N.O.R.E., it got play on mainstream stations, peaking at #32 on the Hot 100 and propelling *Barrio fino* to become the top-selling Latin album of 2005 and of that decade.

Without becoming a major hit on Latin radio, "Gasolina" became the Latin song with arguably the most mainstream appeal since "Macarena," played not only on US mainstream radio, but also all over the world, including in Europe and Japan.

Most important, though, *Barrio fino* and "Gasolina" opened the door for reggaetón's worldwide expansion. Today, the distinctive beat of the music dominates global streaming charts and has put Latin music and artists on the map in a way that was unimaginable a decade ago.

"I had a really different vision," says Yankee now. "I could feel the impact reggaetón was having in the streets, in South America, in the streets of the United States. People were interviewing me even before *Barrio fino*, and I could see what was coming for the entire movement. I knew we were close to exploding. So I said, 'Okay, I'm going to be the one to do it.' And all the money I had, I bet on *Barrio fino*."

The effect of "Gasolina" was profound at many levels. Musically, it ushered a new and distinct genre into the marketplace. Unlike Latin pop or rock, reggaetón, with its recognizable dembow beat, was not a translation or adaptation of something that already existed in the mainstream market. Immediately danceable, it had broad appeal, whether you understood the lyrics or not.

And in terms of business models, Yankee turned out to be a visionary. With reggaetón initially shunned by major labels, he put out the music on his own label, bringing to the table a new ownership model that many artists follow today.

At the end of the day, *Barrio fino* and "Gasolina" ushered in not just a musical movement but a lifestyle, built on a beat with irresistible global appeal that would eventually be the basis for other movements, from Medellín's romantic reggaetón to Argentine trap.

The tipping point, however, was a song about gasoline, conceived by a hungry star on the rise, smack in the middle of a Puerto Rican barrio.

Daddy Yankee

I was in Villa Kennedy [a housing project in Puerto Rico], because I had my studio there. I used to live there with my wife and my three kids. I only did music. It was very spontaneous what happened in Villa Kennedy. I heard a guy outside shouting, "Echa, mija, cómo te gusta la gasolina [Wow, girl, you really like gasoline!]." Song. That's music for you. I thought, "I have to

make a song that has that title—'Cómo te gusta la gasolina.' "
That's what they shout at the girls who are always looking for
a fancy ride to get to parties. I think that's part of the reason
why "Gasolina" was a hit. People were looking for some deep
meaning to the track: Was it about alcohol, about drugs, about
politics? And it's a completely literal subject matter. "Gasolina"
is one of the most wholesome tracks I've written. Luny produced it. The rhythm came from them.

Luny

I started working in Puerto Rico in 2001 and, with Tunes,
started to build a name for ourselves. We started to work on
our own album, *Mas flow* [*More flow*], *vol. 1.*

I'd worked some tracks for [reggaetón duo] Héctor y Tito,
and Daddy Yankee had been featured on one of those tracks. He
liked it a lot and told me, "I'll make a song for your album, and
you can give me five beats for myself and I'll record them." At
the time, if he were to pay me for the beats, it would be around
$2,000 each but he could charge me $20,000 for being in one
of my songs. He already was Daddy Yankee in Puerto Rico. He
and Nicky Jam were the two hottest artists. I was dying to work
with Yankee.

So, he recorded a song for my album. It started, "Métele con
candela, Yankee, métele con candela [Go at it with fire, Yankee,
go at it with fire]." The song is titled "Cójela que va sin jockey
[Grab her she has no jockey]," but really, it's "Gasolina, version 1" because it has the same structure.

It was one of my best songs and that was the first reggaetón
album to cross over into mainstream Latin music. It hit in New
York, and they were playing it in all the clubs. It opened the

doors and I got tons of work. But then Daddy Yankee called, kind of pissed off. "Listen, I need my beat. I already recorded for you and you haven't given me anything."

I took that song, "Cójela que va sin jockey," and I made some quick changes. I gave it to him, he went crazy, he liked it, and he even used the same structure as "Cójela" but with another concept.

Daddy Yankee

I went to Eddie Dee, we started to build the track, and we went back to the Luny Tunes.

I had the chorus and the flows. I record with a lot of flow. Most of the time, I start building the flows, the melodic structure, and then I add the lyrics. When I write hip-hop and rap, the process is different. There I'll sit down and write lyrics first. But with reggaetón, which is more melodic, it's more important to find the hook. In "Gasolina," the chorus was very simple, very easy to remember. The word *gasolina* means "gasoline" everywhere in the world,

Luny

Before, artists would come and ask for a beat. And they would get inspired to write the melody based on that beat. That's what happened with everyone.

He came with his song all ready and done, and from there, we recorded it, adding the production, which took time. I added motorcycles—vroom, vroom, vroom—I added cars. You heard that track and you thought races, cars, gasolina, Fast & Furious.

We always help tweak things. Well, that's what a good producer does: help the artist take his concept to the next level. I told him, "You know, this song is chanteo [chanting] the whole time. We need to give it a break, a little chorus." That's where the line "Tu me dejas algo y no sabes [You leave me something and you don't know it]" came from, where he sings. We helped him take the leap as a singer in that record by adding that break, which is more of a singing voice.

After we recorded it, I spent time with him making changes to the beat, so it would be perfect. I already had the master. But we went back like fifteen times. We'd master it, and then go back and remaster, and, for the time, it sounded really good. When Will.i.am heard that song, he asked me, "Wow. How did you do 'Gasolina'? Where did you mix so that it would sound so big in the clubs?" I did it with Fruity Loops, a program we use that literally costs $100. He couldn't believe it. But that's where we did everything. I still use Fruity Loops to produce.

Daddy Yankee

I changed the beat a bunch of times. *No* one believed in "Gasolina," not even Luny. Because people had gotten used to the classic reggaetón sound. *Barrio fino* is an album that completely changed urban trends. I took out the monotony and opened up people's ears to start to bring different fusions into urban music. Everything [I had made with my two previous albums] *El cangri.com* and *Los homerun-es* I bet on *Barrio fino*.

My wife [Miredys] supported me. Obviously, there are home runs and misses. But I truly had the gut feeling that I wasn't going to fail. That I had the right vision. It wasn't just the song. It was the full movement. I would sit down and watch Premios lo Nuestro, and I would think, "Damn, is this ever boring."

Carlos Pérez

It was 2004. My company was two years old. I had studied design, art, and painting, and I was still working out of my bedroom. I had just finished working on Ricky Martin's *Jaleo* and a friend of mine, Raúl López, kept telling me reggaetón, reggaetón, reggaetón. I wasn't interested. I was living in Miami, so I didn't know a lot about reggaetón. I had done the cover for an album called *MVP*, which included "Dale Don dale [C'mon Don c'mon]," but I didn't even want to credit myself.

I told Raúl the only way I would work for reggaetón is if I work with the Michael Jordan of reggaetón. And he said, "I got the guy. His name is Daddy Yankee."

My office was still in my apartment in Miami and we met there. Milton, Miredys's brother, dropped him off and picked him up. He asked what I did, and I sat down and presented what we could do. It took us like three days, him going line by line and asking, "What is this? Why do I need to do this? Why do I need an ecard?"

Like the website. No artist at the time had a full-fledged website. My impression was someone who was very marketing-savvy. He was a visionary.

Finally, he said, "I want it all. How much does it cost?" Without the video, everything cost about $30,000. It wasn't cheap for the time or for an independent artist. But he just said, "Can you break it down into three payments?"

We worked on the project for like four months. It was the first time an artist, to give them credit, hired me to do everything, the whole package: identity, photography, web, video. We always said that we wanted to come out with the marketing and the identity at the level of any of the top hip-hop artists. We weren't even looking at what was around us in the underground. We were looking at Jay-Z.

My apartment was at the Grand on Biscayne Boulevard in Miami, and that first day, when we had our first meeting, I swear to God, he looked out the balcony and said, "One day, I'm going to own an apartment here." Three years later, he did.

Daddy Yankee

It started with the packaging. I saw that no one had taken the risk to create conceptual album covers. Things in Latin music were cheap. Every time I'd go to the record stores and I bought American music, I saw they spent a lot on the art. That's how I met Elastic People and Carlos asked me, "What do you want to do?" We were both on the same wavelength. We both started from zero. Carlos saw the breadth of my vision and that I wanted to elevate the level from videos to covers to an interactive website.

It cost $30,000, which is a lot. But I went for it, because if I wanted to grow and see this become big, I had to do it. I took out all my savings and I invested them. Carlos also directed my video. We filmed it in the Dominican Republic.

Carlos Pérez

I flew to Puerto Rico and he played me the whole album for the first time as he was mastering. " 'Gasolina,' " he said, "is the smash." I told him I thought he had better songs. And he literally said, "Comprobado por el pueblo. Fui al barrio, le puse la canción a niños y abuelos [Proven by the people. I went to the barrio, played the song for kids and grandparents], and they all love it. This is a guaranteed smash." For the video, he wanted to look "fresh and young." That's why you see him clean-shaven, wearing the white hat.

At the time, MTV allowed four-minute videos. So he took those four minutes and divided it into three songs: "Gasolina," "No me dejes solo [Don't leave me alone]" with Wisin & Yandel, and "King Daddy." At the time it was common to do that; if I'm going to invest money, let's get three into one.

"King Daddy" was the concept song for the Daddy Yankee character, and he felt that "No me dejes solo" and "Gasolina" were the more commercial tracks. The video treatment wanted to embrace speed racing. My dad was in the automotive business, and he told me there was a drag race two weeks later. So we end up shooting in the Dominican Republic and my dad hooks me up with the local drag team. We were shooting on a Monday, after the race. The night before, one of the two cars had an accident in the race, and the driver of the car we were going to use died. In my mind I'm thinking, "At least we have one of the drivers." But the team said, "Listen, we just lost our driver. The other driver is a friend of his and we can't shoot this video. None of our drag racers can go, but we'll send you another car." That's why filmmaking is 90 percent problem solving and fucking 10 percent creativity. They sent a Mustang 5.0 drag, which we didn't see until the day of the shoot.

Because the original video had the other two songs attached, we did "King Daddy" in a comuna [housing project], the "Gasolina" portion at the racetrack, and "No me dejes solo" at the parking lot of the racetrack with Wisin & Yandel.

What pains me the most is that we only shot a minute and a half for "Gasolina." Once the track started picking up, Yankee calls me and asks for a full version of the video, but we didn't have enough material and we didn't have time to go out and shoot more. It was exploding so fast that they took the raw footage and pretty much repeated it. In fact, there's footage in the final video that I would have never used.

Anyway, they repeated the footage. And it just took off.

Gustavo López

Barrio fino came right before we launched Machete, but Universal had the US rights to it through VI Music. I then had a direct negotiation with Yankee, exclusive of VI Music, and we did a worldwide license for *Barrio fino*.

At that time reggaetón was just beginning to explode. A lot of people didn't really know what to do with the genre, and even big artists didn't know what to do with their music outside the United States and Puerto Rico.

There were a lot of things happening around reggaetón, and *Barrio fino* was that landmark release. Yankee must have been teasing *Barrio fino* on prior songs, maybe for two years before. He would be on one record and he would also say, "*Barrio fino*, coming soon!"

Yankee was always very independent. He put a lot of his efforts almost through laser-targeting Puerto Rico and New York, because it was supporting the core markets where he was also doing shows. I take most of the credit for initially believing in the song. I think Yankee knew and Luny knew. Remember, at the time there was no radio for this music. You were going to play in Mega New York and a couple stations in the Northeast. It was Yankee himself who really took the initiative. I can't take any credit for his belief in "Gasolina" or *Barrio fino*. He drove it.

The role that I played was "Oh shit, why is this doing so

well?" I was seeing sales in places where you typically don't see sales. What we did with *Barrio fino* was put it in retail in places it wasn't.

Daddy Yankee

I already had a really different vision. I felt it because of the impact reggaetón was having in the streets, in South America. In the United States, Americans were starting to interview me, even though *Barrio fino* wasn't out on the streets. I could see something was coming for the entire movement, and I thought, "Okay. I have to be the one." What was happening in the streets was coming very strong. The only ones that didn't see it were the labels, who were up there and weren't going to the clubs.

Luny

When we were finishing the album, I was going to release it under my label with distribution from Universal. We went to Miami with Yankee and met with Gustavo López in the lobby of a hotel and I spoke to him about the project. I told him, "This album is going to sell half a million copies." Gustavo said, "You're crazy." I just said it to sell it. I didn't think it was going to be such a big hit. That's why they say you have to be careful what you say out loud because it can become the truth. When the album came out, Gustavo would call me every week and say, "Look, we've sold one hundred thousand! We've sold three hundred thousand! You told us!" After a while we said, "Forget about it. This isn't going to stop."

Daddy Yankee

They started calling me from places like Europe and Japan. It sold platinum in Japan. When the majors found out that I was an indie artist, they all tried to sign me. It was very interesting and at the same time, it was a lesson for me. I had offered *Barrio fino* to the labels before it took off, and no one wanted it. And the ones that gave us reggaetoneros our first break were the American radio stations, not the Latin ones. I made a remix with N.O.R.E. The Power stations were playing reggaetón, because Americans have genres like rap and hip-hop. But for the Latin market, it was something completely new. I understood what was happening because I lived the rap era and I knew it could explode.

Gustavo López

I remember visiting markets and being told by executives in those markets, "This is a great song, but reggaetón will never get played here." The resistance was massive. We live in a world that's all about local repertoire. It's hard enough to bring repertoire from outside, but when you bring an entire Latin movement . . .

Back then there was the English remix of "Gasolina," which might have flown under the radar, but really helped the single out and helped it cross over.

There were two moments that were historic: One was that KISS-FM [an English-language station] added the song in Los Angeles. And then there was a baseball player from Japan who was using the song when he went to bat. And that catapulted the sales in Japan. And then obviously, through Universal, we certainly were critical in pushing the song outside the United States because now we had a license deal.

It really was the song that broke down the doors. "Dale Don dale" and "Gasolina" were the two songs that got crazy airplay on nontraditional stations, and they caused a lot of stations to flip [to a more urban format]. No había quien la parara [No one could stop it].

Carlos Pérez

He had a couple of unique things going for him. He was clean-cut, and he did that very well, knowing he wanted to diversify. And I think the biggest thing was the *Barrio fino* concept. The word alone; it was the first time you put a positive connotation on the *barrio*. *Barrio fino*. The finer things of the barrio. We're going to clean things up and appeal at the level of these hip-hop legends and bring a positive outlook to the genre, which at the time was unique. The photo we used for the cover was the last photo we took that day, at one of the bridges in Key Biscayne. He was wearing a Yankees cap.

Luny

This was the album that marked the history of reggaetón. It took reggaetón to another level, to the level of the Americans. That's what opened the doors for us and everyone knows it. And it's a perfect album—one you can listen to today, and it doesn't sound old. It sounds up-to-date.

Daddy Yankee

Barrio fino is known for "Gasolina," but all of it is a masterpiece, because it brought glamour to the barrio. It placed the barrio at a very high level, and it gave kids the possibility to think, "Wow, if Yankee can, I can."

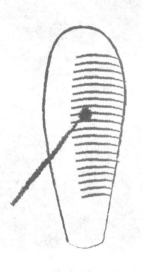

"Vivir mi vida"

Marc Anthony
2013

PLAYERS

Afo Verde: Chairman/CEO of Sony Music Latin-Iberia

Carlos Pérez: Video director

Julio Reyes: Songwriter

Marc Anthony: Artist

RedOne: Songwriter, producer

In April 2013, Marc Anthony premiered a new single, "Vivir mi vida (Live my life)," at the Billboard Latin Music Awards.

The moment was significant for many reasons. Marc Anthony is one of Latin popular music's most enduring icons—a man whose prodigious voice can navigate both pop and salsa with ease and effortless beauty. "Vivir mi vida" was the first single from his upcoming album *3.0*, heralded as his first studio salsa album in a decade. A landmark. Especially considering that poor salsa had fallen way below its heyday. The genre, which had once upon a time dominated Latin music charts and defined Latin music to the world, had been in frank commercial decline since it first seduced Anthony in the 1990s, at the height of its popularity.

It wasn't that tropical music itself had waned, but salsa had, decimated first by reggaetón in the early 2000s and later, by bachata.

"Vivir mi vida" broke the jinx.

The song was a feel-good remake of Algerian singer Khaled's track "C'est la vie (That's life)," originally produced by RedOne and a hit in Europe, the Middle East, and Africa.

The Marc Anthony version borrowed a lot from the original, primarily in its joyful, enhanced-to-sound-like-a-stadium chorus. But Marc Anthony wrote his own lyrics to it, transforming a song about recuperating from a romantic disappointment into an anthem of hope in the face of adversity.

The combination of voice, lyrics, and salsa beat proved to be explosive. "Vivir mi vida" spent eighteen weeks at #1 on the Billboard Hot Latin Songs chart, becoming the first tropical single in a decade to top the chart (and without the aid of remixes), and the longest-running #1 tropical song in history.

By the same token, 3.0, released in the middle of the year, became the biggest-selling Latin album of 2013, according to Nielsen SoundScan.

In an additional nod to his salsa roots, Marc Anthony insisted on filming the video in the East Harlem neighborhood where he grew up, literally in the middle of the street and the middle of his people.

Unlike future smash Latin hits of that decade—like "Despacito," "Bailando," and "Mi gente"—"Vivir mi vida" wasn't a major hit on the Billboard Hot 100, where it peaked at #92.

But that was simply an issue of timing and circumstance. The song was released before mass streaming, which meant the nearly 1 billion YouTube views of the video never got tallied. Perhaps more importantly, Marc Anthony (thankfully) never released a remixed, bilingual version of "Vivir mi vida."

And yet, "Vivir mi vida" single-handedly reignited interest in salsa music, bringing a new legion of fans to the genre. For Marc Anthony, it was an even loftier milestone in a career of milestones, cementing his staying power as he embarked on the longest tour of his life.

For Latin music, it was the beginning of a new, previously unexplored path to globalization. With "Vivir mi vida," Marc Anthony took a track popular in another language and another hemisphere, and reimagined it to the soundtrack of Latin music, multiplying its appeal by a factor of millions. Four years later, J Balvin would do something similar with "Mi gente," only this time, all the mechanisms to measure the global success were in place.

The new Latin Explosion had officially begun.

RedOne

I was in Paris for about a year and met the chairman of Universal France and Canada at the time. We were talking music, this and that, I was playing him stuff, he was happy with all the success. And then he said, "Red, I need to ask you for a personal favor. Do you know the artist Khaled?" And I said, "Yes, he's legend, but we haven't heard from him in ten to fifteen years." And he said, "Exactly. I need a hit. You did it with P Diddy, with Enrique. And I need you to do the same." I said, "I'm honored. I'm a big fan."

I was a little nervous because he had a huge song—"Aicha"

[which was a major European hit in 1996]. I said, "The only thing is, How am I going to top 'Aicha'?" And he said, "Red, you're a hitmaker. You can do it." I spoke to Khaled on the phone; he was excited. At that time I was in Sweden, working, and he said he could come to see me in Sweden. I told him, "Can you come up next week?" The day before he was set to arrive, I knew I had to come up with something. So I did my typical thing. I got my guitar and I started writing. I wanted to come up with something everybody can chant. When you think of things like "Bad Romance," everything is crowd, crowd. I love to have the crowd singing. I started playing the guitar chords [he starts to sing the introduction]. It came up like that, exactly like that. And I wanted to keep the "la la la la," like that. Before he came, I sent him the demo, the whole song without the lyrics, so he could get into it. When he arrived [in Sweden], then we did the lyrics together—me, him, and a few other guys, and we called it "C'est la vie." "We're gonna love each other, we're gonna dance because this is life, la la la la." He said, "I love it, I love it." We recorded, we finished it, and I said to the chairman of Universal, "Oh my God, he is back." And we released it and it was the biggest song in the North African countries, the Middle East. It was the biggest song of his life.

Marc Anthony

A friend of mine, RedOne, he discovered Lady Gaga, and he was on fire with that record. He was also recording with Jennifer [Lopez, who was married to Marc Anthony at the time]. He did a couple of her hits as well, including the one with Pitbull. We became friendly. He became like a brother; just a great friend. One day he was in my house and he said, "Marc, listen to this song. I recorded it with Khaled, and it's called 'C'est la vie.'" I was in the kitchen. I knew it was an anthem right away, because my son Ryan came running up and said, "What song is that?" And he played it again. Not only did I respond to it, but I knew that if Ryan responded to it, there had to really be something special. I put it on again, and Ryan said, "Hold on a second. I have to go get Christian [his brother] because he has to hear this song." Ryan runs upstairs and gets Christian. And he goes, "Christian, Christian, you gotta hear this." And Christian says, "Put it on again, put it on again." And when I saw their reaction, that's when the idea was born. That's when I really knew. That song was almost like butter; it fit in so many boxes.

RedOne

I worked with Marc, and Marc hears everything that I do. And he said, "Red, this song speaks to me. It speaks to me." He was going through a tough moment in his life, and he said, "This is love, this is love." Then his kids came in and said, "Oh my God." And Marc said, "Red, this is a hit. Can I do a Spanish version of it?" I said, "Of course." Because a good song works in any language.

"Brother, it's an honor," I said. If Marc Anthony sings your song, I know it touches you. I thought, "Oh my God, Marc is going to sing this beautiful melody? It's going to touch people." I knew the result was going to be incredible. Marc can almost fool you with a beautiful voice. Even if the melody is mediocre he can make it sound great. But I knew I had a special song.

I told him, "Do your thing." There's such a level of trust between us, that, of course, he listens to what I think, but I know he's not going to make it bad and I understand he's going to keep the melody. Of course, he just did it in a Marc way and made it Marc Anthony with the melody. It's perfect. It's butter to the ears. And it's a beautiful lyric: Voy a reir, voy a bailar, vivir mi vida [I'm going to laugh, I'm going to dance, live my life], la la la la.

Marc Anthony

I was recording my album, I had chosen all these songs, and it was my first meeting with [producer] Sergio George in his studio in Boca Raton. I was on my way to the airport, and although the studio was right there, I'm playing the songs in a car. RedOne had given me the track without vocals and I did a demo of the song [singing] over the track he did for Khaled. It was the pop version. And Sergio says, "That's the first single right there." It was one of those aha moments. I was just so happy.

I said, "I think so, too."

I think we arranged that song in like fifteen minutes, tops. I leaned on Sergio in the beginning because he had a vision for it, and I had no idea how it was going to transition into a salsa song until I heard it.

Julio Reyes

Marc had a song RedOne had given him. It was very funny, because he tells me, "Dokisito [his nickname to me], why don't you translate this?" But it was in Moroccan. The chorus was in French—On va danser, c'est la vie, la la la la la—but the rest was in Moroccan.

I said, "Marc, I don't speak Arabic." But at the time I was very sick. I had a really serious digestive issue going on and I was very vulnerable. And I decided to write the lyrics to the song. I wanted to make this song my declaration of healing. Everything just came together. At the time, the young guys who were building my studio were very Christian. When I walked in there in the mornings, I would find them standing in a circle holding hands and praying. At the beginning, I found it embarrassing, but within a month, I was holding hands with them as well. While they worked, they wrote lines and phrases from the Bible behind the walls of the studio. I found many that were kind of supernatural. And in that context, I started to write the words to the song. In way, it's a little bit like the parable of calming your thirst. I'm referring to the fact that it's built with the architecture of many of the readings of the Bible, especially the parables whose objective is to transcend the mind's judgment and go directly to the spirit. That's what I wanted to do with the words and talk about how everything is so relative. That's the DNA of the song. If you want to make a tragedy of what's happening to you, that's what you'll get. And if you don't, you won't. The DNA of the song lyrics was taking a negative circumstance and trying to make it better. It's funny, because since then I've found out that they sing it in many Christian churches.

Marc Anthony

The Spanish was done between me and Julio Reyes.

I sat down with Julio and his wife, and I told them the lyrics had to be in first person. That was really, really important. The lyrics came from a speech Will Smith gave me. I was filming *Hawthorne* with Jada and we were talking over breakfast and Will was talking about how you have one life to live. That really resonated with me, with where I was in my life. I told Julio, "It has to be about that, but I want to sing it in first person." I felt it would be more impactful. I wanted people to feel it was their story when they sang it. It's their voice. Julio thought that was a great idea.

The message of the original song has nothing to do with "Vivir mi vida." It was about this girl who broke his heart. What made it proprietary was my message. I knew that it was different. The songs I choose to record are usually very in-depth and told from a storyteller's perspective. They're like short novellas. But this was like a short declaration of where I was in my life, and I needed it at that point in my life.

Julio Reyes

It was two days of hard work. One of Marc's big contributions is that the initial approach to the chorus was a little bit preachy. And he told me to make it first person: He said, "Let's write 'I am' instead of 'We are.' Let's eliminate that sense of telling people what they need to do." Instead, we made it about an example to follow. Everything flowed very easily. When it comes to writing lyrics, I tend to be very much an architect, as opposed to a troubadour. But in this case, it came really quickly. And, more than anything, I tried to write in a language that evoked imagery. I think that's what's most effective and what most reaches people. It's a narrative, but it's a visual narrative.

Marc Anthony

I got a lot of pushback with the message. A lot of people who are very important to me, whose opinion I value, when I played it for them, they said, "It's not you. It's not the Marc Anthony we expect. Marc Anthony is not 'la la la, vivir, vivir, bailar, bailar [live, live, dance, dance].'" In contrast to what I had recorded before, it stuck out like a sore thumb. And I thought, "Wow, maybe I lost it. Maybe it's not as special as I think, because the people I really trust are telling me it isn't." It took me like four days where, I wouldn't say I was depressed, but I really doubted myself. Finally, I called everybody in and said, "Sorry, but this is going to be the first single." They said, "This isn't really your DNA, it's your first album in years, it doesn't go with the album." And I just made the call and said, "Everybody can kiss my ass." I was going through what I was going through with Jennifer [Lopez] and life in general. I had to find myself. I had to find myself and what my engine was going to be to be happy.

Did the song help? Yeah, yeah. It became my war cry. You know what? Life is going to happen, no need to cry about it. Sometimes there's a drought, so a rainy day is not always a shitty situation. It's just looking at the positive of everything. Because shit happens it doesn't mean it's the end of the world. Sometimes you need silence to hear yourself think. And that was the impetus.

RedOne

I went to the studio and they played the new version for me. I loved it, but I told Marc, the only thing is the crowd is not big enough. I told him give me the vocals and I have this technique to make it sound like a stadium.

I think I was in Morocco when he sent the final version and I heard it for the first time. I was blown away. I got tears in my eyes. It was very special.

Afo Verde

Marc was coming to our Sony convention. He had just finished the album and had told me he had a song he was crazy about. And because I'm very close to Julio, I had heard that the material was good. So we asked him to come play the entire album for us at the convention, which was your typical convention. The international chairman at the time was there, and his entire staff from London, plus the staff from all the Latin countries. When it came time to play the song ["Vivir mi vida"], Marc said, "I think this is a really important song, and I think it should be the next single." He started the song, and ninety seconds into it I looked around and everybody was dancing. They'd stood up from their tables and they had started to dance. Marc wanted to drive home that "Vivir mi vida" was the single. But the most important thing is, the album was spectacular. And to have such a standout song in a standout album is not easy.

Carlos Pérez

He wanted to shoot in New York. So initially the idea for the video was something like U2 did for "When the Streets Have No Name," which is, let's stage a surprise performance on his block. And let's just document it. So, first of all, when we submitted the permits to the Film Office in the City of New York, they denied the permits. They said, "We will allow you to shoot the video anywhere but on his block. Because he's a star and there's a risk." I had to go back to Bigram [Zayas, Marc Anthony's brother and manager at the time] and Marc, and say we got shot down by the New York Film Office. And they're, "Who, who? Who turned it down?" The New York Film Office is just as powerful as any government entity.

And they said, "We'll be back." And sure enough, they got the permit. Who they spoke to, I don't know, but we got the fucking permit. They said, "We'll give you the permit, but you cannot announce that this is happening." This was 2015 and social media was starting to gain power. We said, "Cool, let's go grassroots." *Grassroots* means knocking on people's doors and saying Marc will perform here tomorrow. The morning of the shoot, call time is like 7:00 a.m and I'm asleep in the car and the producer is driving. He gets a call, and immediately, by the tone of his voice, I know something had happened. I'm like pretending to be asleep, listening to the conversation, but I know some shit went down. I wake up and go, "What's up?"

And he said, "A guy got killed on the corner, and the police have roped off the block." First of all, the body is being picked up, and second, we don't know if there will be retaliation.

Before we even start, it's roped off completely. It's not happening.

Getting Marc early on set is a mission, but he's there. He's there sharp. Our intention was to shoot the video twice, Marc going in and then getting out. But I go to Bigram and I tell him they're not allowing it.

Clearly, there's something going on. There's yellow [crime-scene] tape. People have shown up but are not allowed in.

I tell Bigram, "Unless you have someone above the police chief, he's not allowing this to be an open set."

"What do we tell Marc?" he asked.

"We tell him the truth. Someone got killed."

Now we have a whole production, setup, cameras, label, ready to go. It's not creative anymore. Now it's problem solving.

So I tell Marc, "You know our neighborhood. Someone just got killed. Police are not allowing people in. So we're figuring out what we're doing."

"So, what are the options?" he asks.

And I say, "This is filmmaking. We can stage this shit."
It's a big fucking block. I tell Bigram that we can do one of
two things. We can *not* shoot the video, and shoot another day,
but I have to pay for this. Or we can see if the police allow us
to shoot and we can stage.

We can cast 100 people, or as many as the police allow us to
have. It will require Marc singing the song not twice but more
like ten times so we can arrange the talent around and stage it.
It's filmmaking. It's not the first time we stage something.

Marc Anthony

The video was symbolic as well. I needed to go back to my
roots. I needed to feel like I was owning it again. Everyone in
the neighborhood was "Tony, Tony, Tony." It was symbolic in so
many ways. I needed to go back to where I came from. At that
point, my life was complicated. My lifestyle was complicated,
success was complicated. I just needed to get back.

I remember the shooting situation. I don't remember exactly
the specifics, but I was home.

Carlos Pérez

I told Marc he'll have to sing eight to ten times because we're
going to use the same people and we're going to have to frame
it so it feels full, even though we only have X amount of people.
Marc is in a suit. It's hot as hell. And he's "All right, fuck it, let's
do it."

But Marc is always Marc. He talks to the police and they say,
"We can allow a hundred people, but we have to identify them."
It becomes this whole protocol. Now we're casting people, get-

ting release forms—it's a nightmare. Part of the video treatment said we wanted to document interactivity with el barrio. But when you stage the shit, it's hard to get this authentic feel.

There were hundreds of people standing where the yellow tape was, at the end of the block. So this is what Marc does. He says, "Okay, Carlos, we're going to stage it. How many cameras do you have? I'm going to walk out of this trailer, I'm going to not pay attention to the police, and I'm gonna go say hi to my people. Let's record it all." And sure enough, all the cutaway moments of that video were of Marc literally walking out of his trailer, and the police saying, "Where are you going? What are you doing? If he goes in there, we'll shut it down." And we were just following the artist. And Marc goes under the yellow tape and just immerses himself in the middle of fucking havoc. He's in the middle of the crowd. He's like a superhero in the barrio. They were there because we had gone door to door letting people know that was happening. And, ironically, the reaction was they embrace him, but everyone's well-behaved. All of a sudden, he's taking pictures with kids, taking pictures with older ladies. It was Marc being Marc. It was like five minutes and it felt like an hour. Marc knew exactly what he was doing. All the cutaway moments in the video of Marc in the crowd were five minutes of Marc immersing himself in the people.

The final video starts with an intro, where he walks out of his office. That was the concept. Let's document this moment in history where Marc comes back to his roots. It was like an aspirational message to the people. That's why he leaves the office with these big beautiful views of the skyline, drives through the streets talking this aspirational message, and here is the barrio taking him back.

Marc Anthony

There were people on fire escapes and it reminded me of when I was Tony. And those are my people. It's not like I didn't see that when I was growing up. Circumstances change, but I'm still that guy who walks among my people. I don't even think that's interesting. Of course I would walk among my people.

RedOne

He took it to the level that it's supposed to be. The other version is beautiful, too, but it's another emotion: It's Middle Eastern, French-flavored. I couldn't have been happier to create a historical song with Marc Anthony, who is a brother to me and at the same time, a living legend. I have many hits: "Bad Romance," "On the Floor." But this one was big all over Latin America.

Afo Verde

In Argentina, we're not known for our dancing. But I can almost say Marc Anthony taught me how to dance. He deserves everything that happened with this song.

Julio Reyes

I worked on it as a work for hire. I didn't even think about getting the songwriter credit for the Spanish version. But it's been one of the best gifts of my life, and seeing Marc sing this song at arena shows gives me great satisfaction.

Marc Anthony

I remember never not hearing it after it came out. What stands out about this song is all the doubt that was cast on it at the beginning. That made me doubt myself. Because it had been years and years and I didn't know if I could still compete—salsa had gone out of style. I started doubting myself. But then I had the balls to say, "Listen, I'm not going to doubt myself. This is going to be the first single." Afterward, I asked the same people what the second single should be, and they all said, "Whatever the fuck you say. We'll never doubt you again."

"Bailando"

Enrique Iglesias, featuring Descemer Bueno & Gente de Zona
2014

PLAYERS

Alexander Delgado (Gente de Zona): Artist, songwriter

Descemer Bueno: Artist, songwriter

Enrique Iglesias: Artist, songwriter

Randy Malcom (Gente de Zona): Artist, songwriter

Before "Despacito," there was "Bailando," the Enrique Iglesias smash featuring Cuban singer/songwriter Descemer Bueno and the Cuban duo Gente de Zona. The 2013 track broke all records on the Hot Latin Songs chart at the time by a long shot, remaining #1 on the chart for forty-one weeks. Its closest competition, "El perdón (The loser)" (not coincidentally another Iglesias smash, this one with Nicky Jam), notched thirty weeks at #1, a huge distance from "Bailando."

If "Despacito" broke ground with its mix of reggaetón and pop, raps, and melodies, "Bailando" opened the door to that possibility, marrying Iglesias's up-tempo pop with Descemer Bueno's singer/songwriter vibe and, the coup de grace, the reggaetón beats and gritty vocals of the Cuban duo Gente de Zona. The track was produced by another Iglesias longtime collaborator: Carlos Paucar.

"Bailando" wasn't the first track to marry reggaetón beats to pop sensibility. Already Iglesias had experimented fusing reggaeton's dembow beat with pop in "No me digas que no (Don't tell me no)" and "Lloro por ti (I cry for you)," both featuring reggaetón duo Wisin & Yandel and released in 2009 and 2010, respectively. But the success of "Bailando," aided by a bilingual remix with Sean Paul that propelled the track to #12 on the Billboard Hot 100, paved the way for a new Latin Explosion.

With its mix of pop and urban, English and Spanish, original recording and remix, "Bailando" was the blueprint for the sound that would end up dominating Latin music for the better part of the decade. Likewise, its music video—a cornucopia of dance—would become the first Spanish-language music video to hit the 1 billion viewership mark (to date, "Bailando" stands as one of the ten most viewed videos of all time, even though it was released before streaming truly went mainstream).

In addition, at a time when Cuban artists residing in Cuba had long been absent from the *Billboard* charts, "Bailando" brought them back, with a vengeance; in 2014 Gente de Zona became the first Cuban-based act to ever top *Billboard*'s airplay charts after they were featured on "Bailando."

But it was not a natural progression.

Iglesias wrote "Bailando" with Bueno, a frequent collaborator, in one of many writing sessions the two had in Iglesias's house. The song was placed on hold until Bueno took it to his native Cuba and recorded it with Gente de Zona, a hugely popular group on the island, but little known elsewhere.

After hearing the new version, Iglesias jumped back in and, defying the convention of pairing up with another equally popular act, insisted on keeping Gente de Zona and Bueno in the mix. In that regard, Iglesias was also a trailblazer. While collaboration between stars and lesser-known acts had long been part of the DNA of Latin urban music—a fact that was key in fostering the popularity of the movement—the practice in the pop world was far less common. Almost as uncommon as bilingual remixes.

"Bailando" did it all.

It not only broke ranks; it also opened the floodgates for the creation of a new generation of global Latin hits.

Enrique Iglesias

Descemer and I have known each other and have been writing together since 2005, 2006. The first time we met and started writing at my house, it was weird because I had cowritten songs in English, but I wasn't used to writing together with someone else in Spanish. The first song we wrote together was "El perdedor." Fast-forward, and we wrote a bunch of songs, including "Lloro por ti." I love writing with Descemer. We became like brothers, in the sense that we might not see each other in six months, but we developed a unity there that's difficult to describe. A lot of times you write with other composers, and not that it feels like a job, but it can feel like a nine-to-five task. With Descemer it doesn't feel like that because we write fast and we know we won't be in the same room for more than a few hours. We'll write a bunch of songs at the same time, write a melody, maybe not finish it, and go back and forth. With "Bailando," when he came over and started playing it, the lyrics were not completely finished. He had the verse and what I felt was the chorus, but I felt there was a bridge missing. I said, "Listen, we need to put something in between; we shouldn't go directly into 'con tu física y mi química [with your physics and my chemistry].'" And then I started to sing "Bailando, bailando," but I thought, "Do I want 'Bailando'? I already have a song called 'Bailamos.' Maybe it's not a good idea, but fuck it." I told Descemer that I often think about "Hero," which came out in 2011 when there were other songs called "Hero." So, it stayed the way it was. Carlos [Paucar] produced the track.

Descemer Bueno

This is an idea I had originally conceived as a bachata for Romeo [Santos]. But I took it to Enrique. He liked it, and he asked me not to send it to anyone. That's how we began the song's long journey. Enrique and I started with a basic idea that we began to develop [and rewrite together] and that we changed a lot. [Our version], for example, was a far more acoustic version, and it didn't have that little piece Gente de Zona added later: "Yo quiero estar contigo, vivir contigo, bailar contigo [I wanna be with you, live with you, dance with you]."

We worked for a long time with Enrique on this. He's very good at that . . . at building songs that aren't finished. For example, the chorus of "Bailando" didn't have the phrase "Bailando, bailando." That's something Enrique added, and he wanted it to repeat twice. It took multiple sessions between him and me to get to that part. And the lyrics—tu física y mi química—we worked out together. The thing is, when I took that song to Enrique, he had a million things going on. So we got to a certain point, and it stayed there and we never finished it. Same thing that happens with many songs.

I told him, "Send that song to Don Omar, because I think if Don Omar jumps on this, that song can be really big." He said, "Go for it." We sent it to Don Omar. And what Don Omar did was send us another song called "De noche y de día."

And Enrique completely forgets about "Bailando" and now asks me to help him write the verses for "De noche y de dia." And I suffer. I kept thinking our song was better. But I said, "Okay, let me finish 'De noche y de día.'" Then things got complicated and Don Omar dropped out of that song. And "Bailando" stayed in this sort of limbo. That's when I took the next step with Gente de Zona.

Enrique Iglesias

Descemer and I always have a bunch of songs cooking at the same time, and some take more to write, some take less. I've recorded songs that have been written years ago, but the time wasn't right. In this case, Descemer went to Cuba, he recorded the song with Gente de Zona, and they added the "Yo quiero estar contigo, bailar contigo" line. This is when you realize that a song that makes you feel that there's lightning in a bottle is extremely difficult and all the stars have to align. If Descemer had not taken the song to Cuba and met Gente de Zona, that last part of the song wouldn't have gelled. All the stars aligned.

Descemer Bueno

Months also went by in Cuba. I wasn't really into the urban music scene there, but I did listen to Gente de Zona. I had no connection with them. But there's this young guy who works with them who used to work with me. I had shown him the song many times. And one day he told me, "I know who would be perfect for this song. This group is the hottest thing in Cuba now."

Then I went to my friend's studio—the one who spoke to me about Gente de Zona—but then it was a whole other struggle to get these guys. They were really hot at that point and it was difficult to pin them down. But once they showed up at the studio, there was great enthusiasm.

Randy Malcom

The guy who is now our sound engineer was a friend Descemer and I had in common, and he put us in touch. Descemer was in Cuba and he was hugely popular. He was killing it. We were fans of his songs and we knew the might of his pen. That man writes like God.

Alexander Delgado

We didn't know him, but we knew he was a great composer and that he wrote for a lot of artists. We were fans of his songs.

Randy Malcom

We got together in a restaurant to talk about what we could do together. It's easy for us to fit into other things. He told us,

"There's this song called 'Bailando.'" I said, "Let's go to the studio, let's hear it and let's see what comes out." We went into the studio in Havana and we started to create and create and when we got to the "Bailando" part, Alexander said, "That's my part and no one can touch it."

Alexander Delgado

I said, "I get to sing this part!"

Descemer Bueno

We got together and wrote the "Quiero estar contigo, bailar contigo, una noche loca con tremenda nota [I want to be with you, dance with you, a crazy night with a great groove]," and the "Oh, oh, oh, oh." If it didn't have [those elements], the song would be lacking a very energetic and very important part. But when I heard Alexander sing "Bailando," I said, "There's something here."

Randy Malcom

I started to write that part that says, "Quiero estar contigo, bailar contigo . . ." Then I said, "Maybe we should do another pre-chorus after that chorus." And Alexander began:

"Con esta melodía [With this melody] . . ." And that's how it started coming along, coming along.

Alexander Delgado

When we finished putting that song together in the studio, I said, "That song's going to make me famous worldwide and it's going to make me some dollars."

Randy Malcom

It was something so magical. All these strangers started coming into the studio, and we were so excited by the song, we started playing it for everyone. We even began buying bottles of rum and beer. We put on the song again and again. I think we heard it more than fifty times. I said, "I think we have a song for the ages." We filmed the video [directed in Cuba by Alejandro Pérez], the three of us, before the song was out, and the video became #1 in Cuba in less than a month.

Descemer Bueno

The video came out and everywhere I went, I heard the song. In Miami, if I was stopped at a traffic light and I rolled down my window, the song would play from the homes around me. It wasn't on the radio, but we found out they were playing it in clubs in Los Angeles and we had no idea how. It just spread. And we didn't do a thing.

That "Bailando" in Alexander's voice. I think that was the hook. Enrique liked that. When he finally heard it, he asked, "And that voice?"

Randy Malcom

More than a different sound, we were collaborating with Descemer, who comes from the world of trova. We made the song simply to have a song in Cuba. We did it for ourselves and that's where we lived. We wanted a #1 hit there.

Enrique Iglesias

It's a crazy story because a friend [concert promoter Ernesto Riadigos] called me from Cuba. He was in a taxi, and he said: "I just heard a song called 'Bailando' and I loved it. And your friend is singing."

I said, " 'Bailando'?" Because at the time we didn't know whether to call it "Física y química." And he tells me, "Go check it out on YouTube." I said, "Ernesto, I wrote this song with Descemer!" So I called Descemer and I said, "Descemer, you put out the song and you didn't tell me!" And he said, "Yeah, I was in Cuba, but music you do here stays here [in Cuba]." It was the first time I even heard of Gente de Zona, who I used to call Zona de Gente. It was the mix of so many things that you couldn't plan. The same thing has happened to Descemer and me many times. You can't really plan these things. Whether someone writes something in a song, or they put their vocal on it, suddenly you hear it in a different way. Sometimes it's very difficult to hear music with your voice on it. And when you hear it with other people's vocals, you can be more objective.

Descemer Bueno

It was a whole battle with the label so that they'd leave Gente de Zona in. They said Gente de Zona was a new group no one knew here. That it would be better to procure a bigger artist. Enrique had to fight for them. Those things he considers personal. Enrique has always been the kind of guy who doesn't forget anyone, who doesn't leave anyone behind. He's always been very, very generous with those things. He also fought to have Alejandro Pérez direct the video. He didn't leave anyone behind. Everyone who was involved from the beginning stayed.

Really, there was no reason for me to be in the song. But I imagine he thought it was right for me to have even a small part.

Randy Malcom

Descemer tells us, "Gentlemen, Enrique wants us to jump on the song." We were in Cuba. We couldn't believe it.

Alexander Delgado

When Descemer told us, we didn't believe him. Then we went to a show in Las Vegas. Someone calls me on my cell phone, I pick up, and they say: "Hey, I'm Enrique Iglesias." I thought it was a joke and I hung up. My manager called me and said, "You idiot, Enrique Iglesias is calling you!" I thought it was a machine! Then he called again, laughing his ass off, and we spoke. He said he was very happy to participate in the song, that he'd made the song with Descemer, but they had left it at that, that he really liked what we did with it, and he wanted to be part of it. He said we could tweak anything we wanted except when I sing "Bailando." That was hands-off. He was going to sing the song, but "Bailando" would stay in my voice.

Randy Malcom

Two weeks later we were in Cuba and they sent us the version with Enrique. At that point we said, "Now, this changed. This really changed. Our lives are going to change." No one had ever sung with an artist that big, and definitely not while they were still in Cuba. We knew it would be a revolution. We also knew it was a heck of a song. You feel it when you sing it and when you see people singing it back. You know. It was already #1 in a bunch of places. You know. We had done the earlier video, but when the song with Enrique came in, we took down the original from YouTube. The new one was very similar, but we added scenes with Enrique. But many parts, especially the dancers, were lifted from the original.

Enrique Iglesias

The only thing we did was go shoot the video again with Gente de Zona and Descemer. I probably didn't tell you this, but in [2013] I was at a point musically where I was a bit—I don't know if the word is *saturated*, but I was not as excited when it came to music. And I remember "Bailando" making me feel exactly like I felt when I released my first album. It excited me. It affected me, not only musically; it affected the way I felt. I remember thinking, "Fuck, this is the reason I started to do this, and this is the reason I've been at it for a bunch of years." It's weird to describe.

Descemer Bueno

Alejandro Pérez was the video director. He was a person I trusted and a person I thought could deliver to Enrique in terms of his image. The choreography is by Lizt Alfonso, the most important flamenco teacher in Cuba, and those are her dancers. They deserve a huge amount of credit for the success of the song. The day we shot the video, the main dancer had been sidelined because she was overweight. The director spotted her in a corner and asked, "Why are you there all alone?" And she said, "I've been taken out because I'm fat." He asked that they lift her suspension so he could do some screen tests. Then they added the story between Enrique and the girl, which gave the video a lot of strength. There was chemistry between them on-screen and he's not easy for those things. He's very finicky.

Enrique Iglesias

It just made me feel extremely happy. I remember meeting with Republic Records. We had released a single that didn't do as well, and Monty Lipman and Charlie Walk came and told me, "Well, we just put out a single, and it didn't do so well. What else do you have for us?" This was backstage at Madison Square Garden. I remember telling Monty, "There's this song in Spanish that I do feel could be the best song I've ever done in Spanish." And he said, "Play it for me." After he heard it, he said, "Translate that shit."

And I thought, "How the hell am I going to do that?" I had done translations before, but I knew this was a translation that could make or break it in the Anglo market. I'm not good at translations, because I believe if a song is written in Spanish it should be in Spanish, and if the song is in English it should be in English. And I thought to myself, "Dude, shut up. There are no rules." So I translated the song and wrote all the lyrics in English. After a month of Monty and Charlie up my ass, I called Sean Paul. I knew he would get it. He was good at adding to songs that maybe were not in English, but he made them sound great.

Randy Malcom

No one had an issue in Cuba. On the contrary. It was a total revolution. For us to step onto the *Billboard* platform, as Cubans who lived on the island, was incredible. It was something no one thought would happen, in a million years. We went to the Billboard Latin Music Awards and we were rehearsing the song. And the presenter said, "Enrique Iglesias, with his song 'Bailando'!"

Enrique stopped the rehearsal and said, "No. It's not just my song. I need you to introduce Enrique Iglesias, Gente de Zona, and Descemer Bueno." He gave us the respect others weren't giving us. He put the cards on the table.

That song completely changed our lives.

Descemer Bueno

The song came out on April 16, 2013. One of these days I'll start celebrating the birthday of "Despacito." Because it feels like my birthday. Without "Bailando" there would not have been a "Despacito." It's a song that's become a point of reference. Many songs came after it that had the same harmonies, similar rhythms, similar rhythmic touches. It really was a winning formula. It's the kind of song that will never stop being played. It still sounds current. Obviously, it's not like we invented anything. We found a harmonic structure that doesn't belong to anyone. But maybe, up until that moment, it wasn't what was being sought out.

Enrique Iglesias

I didn't realize the full impact until months later, a friend of mine sent me a song by Nicky Jam, called "El perdón." I thought, "Shit, this is so good." And I realized he's using a lot of the chord progressions of "Bailando." I thought it was genius in the sense that you could tell he was inspired by it. But I thought I have to ask him in person. And when I met him, I said, "How did you guys come up with 'El perdón'?" He said, "Honestly, I was listening to 'Bailando' and we came up with 'El perdón.'"

I think I see "Bailando" opening more doors to other collaborations. Let me put it this way. If I didn't have "Bailando," "El perdón" would have never fallen in my hands. If it wasn't for "Bailando," the genre would not have gone where it went.

"Bailando" made me love music again. It motivated me to go back in the studio and not forget about what got me there. It's all about the song. It's not about you. It's really about the song.

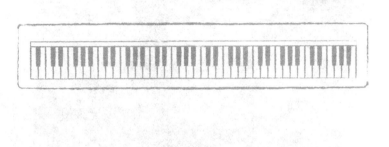

"Despacito"

Luis Fonsi, Featuring Daddy Yankee & Justin Bieber
2017

PLAYERS

Andrés Torres: Coproducer

Carlos Pérez: Video producer

Daddy Yankee: Artist, songwriter

Erika Ender: Songwriter

Jesús López: Chairman/CEO of Universal Music Latin America & Iberian Peninsula

Juan Felipe Samper: Justin Bieber's Spanish-language vocal coach

Luis Fonsi: Artist, songwriter

Mauricio Rengifo: Coproducer

Monte Lipman: Chairman/CEO of Republic Records

Scooter Braun: Justin Bieber's manager

Movements are never the product of a single action.

And yet many of the recent developments in Latin music are labeled *pre-* or *post-*"Despacito."

In the summer of 2017, this juggernaut of a song reigned at #1 on the Billboard Hot 100 chart for an astonishing sixteen weeks, tying the record for most weeks at #1 that had been long held by Mariah Carey and Boyz II Men's "One Sweet Day" (the record was finally broken in 2018 by Lil Nas X with "Old Town Road").

"Despacito" would become the most listened-to song in the world and the original video (one with Bieber was never filmed) would go on to become the most viewed ever on YouTube. More importantly, it would open the floodgates for a wave of Spanish-language and Latin-themed tracks, which would permeate not just the *Billboard* charts but global awareness as a whole. Today we no longer talk about the next "Despacito," but about an ongoing Latin music movement.

Despite the seemingly immediate cause-and-effect proposition of "Despacito," the song and its impact—after all, this book is partly inspired by it—were the result of a long slow boil that was years in the making, both musically and culturally. By the time "Despacito" came along, the global appeal of Latin music in general, and reggaetón beats in particular, had been proven time and time again. But "Despacito," which was undeniably a great pop song, also arrived at a time when streaming services truly came of age. For the first time ever, the global consumption of Latin music could be very precisely measured, and the world was able to see the rise of a song, in Spanish, through the ranks of the YouTube and Spotify global charts.

The success of Latin music was no longer anecdotal. It was real.

Released January 13, 2017, "Despacito" was originally

recorded by Puerto Rican crooner Luis Fonsi, featuring reggaetón star Daddy Yankee, and produced by Mauricio Rengifo and Andrés Torres, two bilingual Colombian producers. The song debuted at #2 on the Hot Latin Songs chart on February 3 and went to #1 just three weeks after its release. It rose to #3 on Spotify's global chart, unprecedented for a Spanish song, and the video climbed to #1 on YouTube's Global Music chart, surpassing Ed Sheeran. But come April, the track had risen only as far as #48 on the Hot 100 in the three months since its January release.

Then came the Bieber remix. Within a week, "Despacito" jumped to #9, then #4, #3, and, on the May 24 chart, #1.

Keep in mind it took Bieber for the United States to really take note of "Despacito," even as the rest of the world devoured the song in its original Spanish-only version. This underscored the difference between non-Latin countries like the United States and England, where playing a song in Spanish was still a fluke, and a global streaming market, where Latin music had become more mainstream.

"Despacito" pushed the door of possibilities wide open. If "Livin' la vida loca" provided the tipping point for the Latin Explosion of 1999, "Despacito" was the catalyst for a new version that didn't necessarily have to rely on English to cross over.

"Two and a half years later, what really hits me is the fact that it opened a huge door for the non-Latin world to vibrate to Latin music," Fonsi told me recently. "It spearheaded a global Latin movement. I want to stress that I don't mean to say it was all me or the song; it was the sum of many songs and many artists. But this song definitely kicked the door open."

Luis Fonsi

[The day I wrote it], I woke up with "des-pa-ci-to" in my head. It was so loud and clear that I had to research if this was already a song I might've heard before. I then ran to my home studio, powered it up, picked up my guitar, and started recording. I wanted to make sure I wasn't going to forget it, because I felt there was something interesting in the simplicity of it. I had the main blueprint of the chorus all before my morning coffee. That afternoon I had a writing session scheduled with my dear friend Erika Ender. As soon as she walked in, I sang the chorus idea and she got it right away.

Erika Ender

I went to his home in Miami around 2:00 p.m., we had a cafecito, and then we went into his studio and he said, "Since this morning, I've been mulling writing a song called 'Despacito.'" Usually when people cowrite, someone brings the original idea to the table. He sang the first line for me. And the second: "Vamos a hacerlo en una playa en Puerto Rico." And I said, "Hasta que las olas griten, 'Ay bendito' [Until the waves shout, 'Oh Lord']" [laughs].

From that point on, we began to build the song, moving the Puerto Rico line to the end, so it wouldn't sound so regional, and creating a story. We worked with Fonsi on guitar, looking for the right melodies. In fact, I have the original sessions recorded. Whenever you're in a session, you record as you go; at least that's my technique. I like to go back to the top to create a story. It was also about getting [Fonsi] out of his comfort zone. Because people know him as a balladeer, but he's an incredibly versatile artist and he's totally credible. He sings, he dances, he writes.

Luis Fonsi

It [ended up being] one of the first songs on the album. I did a demo with my guitar. Then Erika came in, we wrote the song, I wrote the choruses, did the demo top to bottom, and kept working on the album with this experiment called "Despacito" that I had in my back pocket. I knew I had a song, but I felt it needed something. I didn't know whether to leave it as a pop cumbia or add another beat. At the time, the album still didn't have an identity. In fact, we have a more pop version of the song.

Erika Ender

A song has to be like a marriage of words and music, and it needs an easy-to-understand story that will grab the listener. Something that makes you say, "This song is for me" or "It's something I can dedicate." That's what we did with "Despacito": Create a story that would put the woman in the place she deserved to be. I was trying, with the lyrics, to say how I like to be treated. We like to be treated despacito, to be wooed despacito. We live in such an immediate time, where sex always comes first and women are treated as objects. So it was a little bit about inviting people to live more slowly, to conquer women in a different way. I don't have issues with any musical style, but I do have issues with messages that aren't positive for humanity. We were really excited as we wrote. So much that I posted a Facebook Live and said, "We have a hit!"

Luis Fonsi

I give a lot of credit to Andrés and Mauricio. I met Andrés years ago. I used to hire him to record demos for me in Los Angeles [where Rengifo and López are based] when I wrote with [composer] Claudia Brant. While Claudia and I wrote, [Andrés] would record the tracks. Then we started to write together. And finally I asked him to produce songs for my album. He told me, "I have a partner, Mauricio." So they came to my house in Miami and stayed with me for ten days. The last day, I said: "Guys, listen to this." And I put on the demo for them. And telepathically, because those two communicate without speaking, they both said, "Dude, that's reggaetón." And they started to edit it there, and that was that. I'd say 90 percent of the track you hear today was done in my house in two hours.

Mauricio Rengifo

When Fonsi first played the demo for us, it didn't have reggaetón, which is a big part of what made the song so easy to listen to. But it did have "Despacito," which is a golazo [touchdown] and a fantastic idea. We were working on Fonsi's album and would periodically get together and work on the song. It took a long time to get it done, not because it took a long time to write, but because of the bureaucracy involved: Who would be featured? When would they record? There was a lot of trial and error. But that's one of the song's virtues. We had time to work on it.

Luis Fonsi

Afterward, we started to fine-tune it. What can we add that really has that Puerto Rican flavor? There's no more Puerto Rican instrument than the cuatro. So we called Christian Nieves, a very well-known cuatro player on the island. I had met him because Tommy Torres uses him a lot. He knows how to fuse a very traditional instrument into a pop song. I asked him to add cuatro to the song, and about two days later, he sent me a take he recorded in his studio in Puerto Rico. By then, Andrés and Mauricio had gone back to Los Angeles. We took that and put it on the track. When we finished, there's a cuatro line in the chorus that, to me, was what brought it all together; it's the star of the show.

There were several turning points in the song. The day I wrote it with Erika. The day I wrote with Andrés and Mauricio, when we realized it was different from anything else. When we added the cuatro. After that, we mixed the song, and that's when I said, "Uf, it needs a feature." It needed that moment of explosion in the second verse.

Mauricio Rengifo

Initially, Fonsi had asked Nicky Jam to record, and he did. But there was a conflict with the release of his own album, so Nicky suggested Fonsi call Daddy Yankee.

Daddy Yankee

Fonsi sent me an email and said, "Yo, I have this crazy song." Obviously he's the creator and main author. But there was something missing in the song. I came to the studio and I did my thing: the verse and the pre-hook, "pasito a pasito [step by step]," that was my creation. The ending of the song was also very different. I told Fonsi we needed to repeat "pasito a pasito" after the bridge. He gave me a lot of liberty.

Luis Fonsi

When Yankee came in, we went to record at Criteria [a well-known recording studio] in Miami. I was there the whole time when we worked. He wrote his part at that moment. Obviously, I had sent him the song, but he created his part right there and we recorded it. From Criteria, we went to my house to edit Yankee's vocals and add them to the track, and that was the last turning point. That's when I said, "Holy shit. Yankee gave it that energy." I don't have that in my voice. Yankee's a hype man. He has that ability to get you out of your seat. Combined with my approach, which is more melodic, it was the winning combination.

Mauricio Rengifo

The song really took shape 100 percent when Yankee recorded. It was 2:00 a.m. when we went to Fonsi's house and listened to the track for the millionth time, and yes, we felt musically it was where it had to be.

Erika Ender

I also loved what Yankee added. The song went through several arrangements, and I have to give Fonsi credit, because he went into the studio with the producers until he got exactly the arrangement he wanted. All the planets aligned. It's like pieces on a chessboard, placed there by the universe. None of us imagined this would have such impact. We knew we had a hit, but we had no notion of how quickly it would come.

Luis Fonsi

The video is exactly what I wanted to portray the day I picked up my guitar with the original idea. It's a song with a Latin essence, that makes you want to dance, that represents my memories of Puerto Rico, where I grew up. That, to me, is the video, and that's how we conceived it. I called Carlos Pérez, who's a friend, and I said, "This is what I want. I want a video that's not cliché, no piña coladas. I want a Puerto Rico that's rawer." And between the two of us, we started to create.

Carlos Pérez

One day [Luis] calls me and says, "I have this song that is going to be my next single and I want you to do the video. It's something very Puerto Rican and I want to work with a Puerto Rican director. I want it to be authentic. It's with Nicky Jam and it has an urban beat. I'm going to send you the demo. Check it out and call me back." The bigger challenge was how to make a video for Luis Fonsi with an urban track that's credible. I got writer's block.

I [finally] wrote the first "Despacito" treatment. I knew it was a little bit out there. I think it was like a movie. The girl was a dancer or a bartender, and they're both trying to romance her, and at the end she leaves with a girl, I think.

Fonsi reads it and calls me and says, "I appreciate it, but, you're overthinking. I want Puerto Rico, I want bright colors, I want a sensual girl, I want dancing, I want barrio." Then, while I'm in the process of writing the second treatment, he calls me and says [Nicky couldn't do it because his own single was coming out]. A week later he sends me the demo with Daddy Yankee. The new version, with the "pasito a pasito" part, puts you at a party, which the original did not. I think that was what creatively Yankee brought to the party. I tell Fonsi, "Well, you had a good song. Now you have a fucking great song."

Universal obviously supported it and Fonsi needed that. He was Universal's pop star who had been a little passive. Everyone knew the importance of the track.

Luis Fonsi

We went to La Perla [a Puerto Rican seaside barrio in San Juan, known for its colorful houses]. We had the dance element, but we didn't want a choreography that was "Fonsi and his dancers." We wanted like a *Dirty Dancing*, Latin style. That dance style isn't cheesy, but it's like going into one of these hole-in-the-wall places in Puerto Rico or New York and you begin to dance. Everything was carefully planned. Then the model. I didn't want just any model. It had to be *the* model. It's not a video that has a lot of kissing or passion. There's a lot of flirting. Again, it was very carefully planned. I called Zuleyka [Rivera, former Miss Puerto Rico and Miss Universe]. She loved the song. Everything fell into place. Even the guy who shouts in the song. I had asked my percussionists to be extras on the set, and we started this party impromptu. I told Carlos to open the mike and record their shouts and it ended up being part of the video. We made a party, even though it's not on the song recording.

Carlos Pérez

There were two things I felt strongly about from the outset. One was, we needed to shoot in La Perla to convey what Fonsi and Yankee wanted. And when I wrote it, I felt Zuleyka was the person. I was very convinced she was the one who could pull it off, because she's obviously beautiful, but also, because I knew she had a dancing background. There's nothing more dangerous than going to a shoot with a model who can't dance.

The one unique factor in this shoot, compared to any other one, is that the vibe of the song would stick to the talent, the crew, the bystanders. Everyone was engaged. I had never felt that way in a shoot. What you see in the video is exactly what was felt.

It's not my most artistic video, but it's the most honest video in terms of the song.

Jesús López

I wanted it to be the first video and single to be released in 2017 and I pressured the team to have everything ready to go before the Christmas holidays. No one could predict what happened. Radio really wasn't waiting for a Luis Fonsi track. Yankee's contribution was crucial for the song to expand artistically, and later, both the video and social media were key elements in delivering an amazing kickoff that revved up traditional media, radio, TV, and press.

Luis Fonsi

Probably about a month after its release I realized that this was going to be a game changer for me. The response was instantaneous. I was now doing promo in markets where my music had never been played before, places where Latin music in general rarely gets played.

Jesús López

By the end of January, we were seeing numbers we just hadn't seen before. We always had a remix in mind, but failed in our initial efforts to find an Anglo artist, until Justin Bieber heard the song at a club in Bogotá [Colombia]. At that point, I knew the last and most difficult barrier was going to fall. We at last had the chance to be #1 in the United States and the UK, and I knew that would unleash a global domino effect.

Scooter Braun

"Despacito," when Justin jumped on it, was already a big song in the Latin world. Then it went crazy. I was frustrated hearing on the news the president of the United States talking about Mexicans and Latinos the way he was talking about them. I got offered to do the remix of "Despacito" with one of my clients and the client didn't want to do it, so I said, "Justin, why don't

you get on it?" He was down in Bogotá and he heard "Despacito" in a nightclub and he said, "Man, the girls went crazy.
Should I do this?" And I said, "Yes. But if you do it, you need
to do it in Spanish." And he goes, "But I don't speak Spanish."
And I said, "Yeah, but you can mimic anything. And I think
it's really important that people hear you sing in Spanish and
they're going to go crazy." He said he'd do it and I flew an engineer down [to Colombia] to record.

Juan Felipe Samper

Bieber was performing a show in Bogotá, and I got a call asking
to meet with his team because they needed a translator. They
didn't say what they wanted me to translate. I met them at the
W Hotel and they told me to go to a recording studio the following day and that only two people would be there: me and the
sound engineer. They were flying in Justin's engineer from New
York. They just told me to go and wait, and around 2:00 p.m.
I got a message saying Justin was on his way. He arrived with
two friends and said, "Have you heard a song called 'Despacito'?
Here's what we're going to do. [Producer] Poo Bear is going to
send me the lyrics to the song in Spanish and I need you to be
my vocal coach and make sure my Spanish is correct." It was
both exciting and stressful. I'd done vocal coaching in Spanish
before, but never in another language. The first thing I thought
of doing was something I'd done with [songwriter] Jorge Luis
Piloto, who translated songs for Mariah Carey: He wrote the
songs phonetically in English, so she could just read in her own
language. So, I wrote it out and said, "Read this: *des-pah-zee-
toh.*" We worked on the diction for around half an hour and
then we started to record. When he finished, he walked out
of the recording booth, he gave me a hug, and he told me he

loved how we had worked. It was an amazing experience. As if Michael Jackson had invited me to record "Thriller."

Luis Fonsi

It took four days between when he heard it and when it was out. What many people don't know is there's a full English version of the song. But he said he wanted to do his own version.

He added an extra layer to the song. Sometimes you hear remixes and it's different or you go to the original. He was very smart in that it started with his voice. Because your regular listener doesn't know who Daddy Yankee and Luis Fonsi are. And that was very smart.

Juan Felipe Samper

When we went into detail, the toughest words were *pasito a pasito*. For us it's easy, but they [non-Spanish speakers] have a hard time hearing the *a* in between the two words. And "Para que te acuerdes [so you remember]" was the toughest, because he couldn't hear the *a* at the beginning of *acuerdes*.

Monte Lipman

We have a very close, long-standing relationship with Jésus and his team. When "Despacito" broke, we knew there was an opportunity to cross the record and we knew a remix was necessary to go to the English-language stations. Scooter Braun called me on a Tuesday and said, "This record you spoke to me about—Bieber loves it, but the caveat is, he wants it out in forty-eight hours." You're talking recording the record, mixing the record, mastering. We had to fly someone down to South America that day to record vocals. Had we attempted to cross the original version, we still would have achieved a certain level of success. But when you add someone like Justin Bieber to the record, you create an event. Based on the immediate reaction in the marketplace, anything less than a #1 record was unacceptable. The way we saw it, the universe spoke. What Fonsi and Yankee did was exceptional. Bieber was the hot sauce. And it eliminated any excuses of anyone who said they couldn't play the record.

Scooter Braun

When I sent the record to radio, I had American programmers call me and say, "It's too much Spanish." It's supposed to be a crossover record for him. And even Luis Fonsi will tell you, he wanted us to go back in. I said, "Hell no." Mike Chester was my head of radio at the time. I said, "Mike, tell them to play it for two weeks. If it doesn't work in two weeks, we'll go back and do more English." Obviously, we went for two weeks and it went to #1 for sixteen straight weeks. I didn't expect that to happen. I wanted to be #1 for a week. Then it went to #1 for the entire summer of Trump's first summer in office.

Mauricio Rengifo

The big success of having Justin, beyond the marketing, of course, is that, as a songwriter and performer, he approached the song from a completely different point of view than that of reggaetón or Latin music. His first verse was totally different from what any Latin act would have done. It was very impressive and very cool for all of us to hear him do what he does. His approach to American music and melodies worked so well on a track that wasn't conceived for the Latin market.

Andrés Torres

[In response to criticism of Bieber singing in Spanish:] The fact is, Justin Bieber is singing a song in Spanish and it's #1.

Mauricio Rengifo

The fact that he made an effort to sing in Spanish is a sign of respect toward our culture and our language. If he didn't care, he wouldn't have done it in Spanish. Or he would have said, "Despaciro." But he respects Spanish so much that he recorded in Spanish. That's vital.

Erika Ender

It was a great song, with a great arrangement, at a time when Latins were making a splash with reggaetón, which is no longer reggaetón. Now it's pop fusion. People were going back to dancing and feeling the rhythm. But you also need a message. And I think "Despacito" has a message. Despite its sensual or sexy tone, the way it conveys the message makes all the difference. It was the coming together of a moment with a great song with Bieber getting on board and it opened many doors.

We're at a time when Latin stopped being Latin and began being cool.

Luis Fonsi

It's a song I've performed on every continent on the planet. In places that are very culturally different from us: the Middle East, Asia, Russia. Places far removed from our way of dressing, dancing, feeling, moving. And still the song managed to cut through everything.

Today, a song like "Despacito" is normal. But four years ago, when I mixed this cumbia with guitar, with a Puerto Rican cuatro used for traditional Christmas music; when we brought together a pop act with the king of reggaetón; when a remix with Justin Bieber happened. All of that sounds normal now. But back then it wasn't.

"Mi gente"

J Balvin and Willy William
2017

PLAYERS

Anthony Belolo: President of Scorpio Music

Fabio Acosta: J Balvin's comanager

Harold Jiménez: Cofounder of 36 Grados

J Balvin: Artist, songwriter

Jean Rodríguez: Diction coach

Jesús López: Chairman of Universal Music Latin America & Iberian Peninsula

Rebeca León: J Balvin's former comanager

Willy William: Artist, songwriter

The year 2017 ushered in the new Latin Explosion. The unexpected success of "Despacito" was so huge and so sudden that it initially felt like a fluke. But then came "Mi gente." J Balvin's reimagining of French DJ Willy William's "Voodoo Song," released in April 2017, had the makings of a global hit—from its conception as a song that brought together global influences and roots to its edgy execution. It rose quickly through the charts, and by August 1, it became the first-ever all-Spanish-language song to hit #1 on Spotify's global chart. For Balvin, the Colombian star who had reconfigured urban music with an edgy, global aesthetic, it was validation. Just a year before, he had predicted that Latin acts would no longer need to "cross over" by singing in English in order to reach global #1s.

But "Mi gente" had other heights to reach. On September 28, Beyoncé posted a twenty-second snippet of something on Instagram with a rather cryptic caption: "I am donating my proceeds from this song to hurricane relief charities for Puerto Rico, Mexico, and the other affected Caribbean islands." By the following day, more than five million people who clicked on the link heard their queen sing in Spanish, in a remix of "Mi gente."

"Mi gente" never made it to #1 on the Hot 100, as its cousin "Despacito" did. But in October, the remix of the song featuring Beyoncé reached #3 on that chart, while "Despacito," featuring Justin Bieber, sat at #9. It was the first time in history that two mostly Spanish songs had simultaneously made the Top 10. Even in 1999, at the height of the Latin Explosion, Ricky Martin, Enrique Iglesias, and Jennifer Lopez had shared Top 10 placement on the chart, with their English tracks.

The success of "Despacito" and "Mi gente" highlighted a different kind of Latin Explosion—one that underscored a shifting demographic and a global appetite for Latin beats, for the first time easily consumable via streaming services worldwide.

Beyoncé would subsequently invite Balvin to perform in

Coachella with her, laying the groundwork for his own head-lining performance that year, the first time ever that a Latin act headlined the event.

By the following year, Balvin's quest to take Spanish music global continued to progress as he performed at the Super Bowl halftime show, marking the first time ever that an artist who did not record in English performed in that slot.

Willy William

I started writing this song around October 2016. I was working on different projects and, as many artists do, looking for sounds, looking for patterns, for drum kits, for a hook. In the process of doing that, I got into synths and loops and found this sound [the instrumental introductory hook to "Mi gente"]. It was special. It sounded really good.

The thing is I was working on different projects with different BPMs and elements, but I gave up the project I was working to focus on this hook, adding my voice to it, pitching my voice on it, spending one hour on it, and finally it became the hook to "Voodoo Song." I added some percussions, some drums, and after maybe three hours, I was standing with the final instrumental "Voodoo Song" before I added vocals to it. I didn't touch the track after that. I simply added the topline. And the thing is, when I finished the instrumental of "Voodoo Song," every part of my vocals came really quickly. I was very, very inspired by the hook, by the instrumental.

Before "Voodoo Song" and "Mi gente," I was working on fringe stuff.

It took me a long time to realize that it was good because I was focused on different things. But when I started to send it to a couple of my close friends, they said, "Man, you got something really crazy." And then we did the dancing chicken video. I was in Miami for a different purpose and I missed my flight and I was stuck in a hotel and I decided to put fifteen seconds of "Voodoo Song" on a video of a twerking chicken I found on a link. I edited, dropped it on social media, and forty-eight hours later, when I was on the flight back to France, everything went super viral. I got 40–50 million views on Facebook until they blocked it because it showed a twerking animal. This was months before the official release of the song.

Anthony Belolo

The song was big in France already and we had a dream with Willy where we wanted a Latin collaboration. We had heard J Balvin's "Ginza" and thought of him to do a Latin version of our song. We contacted Fabio [Acosta, Balvin's comanager], and he immediately answered and it went super fast.

Fabio Acosta

The first time I heard about anything French-related, we were in Paris—I think at the Chanel event in December 2016. José [J Balvin] said, "Let's find the hottest artist in France." And that was that. And later we were in New York driving somewhere, and he said, "Check out this song. It's by a French DJ called Willy William and I already called him and we're going to record it." José is like that about his music. He's his own A&R.

J Balvin

Mohombi [a Swedish Congolese singer and DJ] sent me the original song by Willy William in French. I was at home when I first listened to it. The beat made me say, "This is a megahit." I blindly believed it would be a global hit. I said, "Let's do it, but let me write the chorus, in Spanish, and let me write the verse, in Spanish, because I think it has all the elements of a great hit." The record was already out in French and Willy was a little doubtful of the version I was giving him, because it was a new version, not a remix.

Willy William

My team from Scorpio started the legal negotiation, and Balvin and I got in touch through Instagram. Everything was very natural. He wrote me something and I realized it was Balvin writing me on Instagram. I thought maybe it's not the real Balvin. I replied something, but I wasn't really convinced. I thought, "Okay, I'm talking with J Balvin. Crazy." But at the same time my guys in Scorpio were having their boring conversations.

Jesús López

We came to an agreement with Willy William's label, Scorpio, and closed a deal that made sense to us and gave us control of the track. We thought it would be a huge hit.

Fabio Acosta

José discovered the track and then we invited Willy William to Miami to record and film the video. They came with the notion of recording in English or French, and José said, "No, no, no. We're going to break this in Spanish." Willy William's part is entirely in Spanish. That was key. They wrote those lyrics that night in Miami—at a studio in Doral that belongs to the father of [singer] Tomas the Latin Boy. It was like 1:00 a.m.

J Balvin

It was key that the entire song be in Spanish. I knew what would connect. I knew the time was right and there were a lot of things going on in the world. "Mi gente" is actually a love song. It's all about no discrimination for my people. We recorded Willy William's verse in Miami and the next day we filmed the video. He was still a little bit hesitant, but I told him to trust, that I knew what I was doing. But he was doubting. He thought his version was going to be the hit, which I respect. But we were going to win one way or the other. If this one didn't work, his version would work. But he finally believed and he followed my lead completely.

I had that certainty and that faith, that intuition that doesn't fail me. I think it's a gift from God and the universe. The rest, of course, is history. The song became a hymn of the planet, of DJs, of clubs. It's a song about inclusion that's for everyone. For mi gente, my people. All races, all colors, all genres, all genders, all sexual orientations. It's a song that's 2,000 percent inclusive and is an anthem of tolerance.

Rebeca León

He recorded it in Spanish. He had a vision. I want to take this song, I want to do it in Spanish. It's going to be huge. He was so clear. He knew it.

Willy William

We finalized the package in forty-eight hours—one day in the studio and one day for the video. It was my first experience running things this way. It was my first big international experience and my first big collaboration. I learned a lot from scratch to right now and I'm still learning a lot.

Balvin and I met in the studio for the first time, but it was like I saw him yesterday. We spent maybe one hour talking about everything, to catch the vibe and set the mood. And after that, everything came really naturally. And you can feel it in the song.

I believe 100 percent in karma and the universe and there are no coincidences. It's all about perfect timing.

Anthony Belolo

The biggest challenge was that when we arrived in Miami to meet José, we were supposed to go to the studio with Willy, but we were jet-lagged. Willy's voice wasn't sounding as good, and we did the session, but we weren't too happy about it. When we got to the hotel, at the last minute, we booked a studio for first thing in the morning because we had to be at the video shoot at 8:00 a.m. We jumped in a cab at five in the morning and we rerecorded the song, Willy's lyrics and Spanish. We didn't have the final track until we arrived at the video set with the new version in hand three hours later.

Willy William

When we met, I didn't have time to be impressed, because it was forty-eight hours of intensity. I was supposed to deliver the final version after the studio session, and instead of sleeping, I was mixing the track until seven in the morning. And we had to be ready at 8:00 a.m. for the first shoot. That's why this period was really intense. It was forty-eight hours of intensity. The jet lag, plus the pressure.

J Balvin

I told them we had to make a video that would really make a difference. Something that anybody, anywhere, of any race could understand. We wanted it to show a lot of Colombia, but in a cool way, without going too folk. And if it did go folkloric, we had to find a way to make that cool, because folk can be cool. But the main thing was to have a visual document that everybody could understand without having to think too much about it. And do that with a totally cool look. And we achieved that.

Harold Jiménez

We had already worked with José on several videos before. This time, he'd bought his first plane and he invited us to travel with him to an awards show. We are chatting, listening to new music, and one of the songs was "Mi gente." The song was Willy William's, but José took it and transformed it completely. But the moment we heard it [the original], the energy was, like "uf." It was just really good. It made us move our heads. So much so that we held to that, and in the video, we make people move their heads. It sounded different from other reggaetón songs at the time. José always demands a lot of us. Every time we do a video for him, he tells us, "Forget everything we've done before. This is going to be our first video and we have to go all out." He always puts that pressure on us. With "Mi gente" he also said, "We have to break it. This song is different and we have to break it."

In 36 Grados, we work as a team, and the ideas don't come from a single person. We sat down with the team and started to toss ideas around, and look for those characteristic elements of our culture to include in the video. The figures painted on the background when José sings, for example, are inspired [by] the molas [colorful handmade textiles], traditional figures of the Colombian Pacific coast.

We have a palenquera—those Afro-Latina women of Cartagena who dress in colorful dresses—but we gave her a designer outfit and placed her in a plaza in Medellín. And when you see José on a bus with the Colombian flag, the original idea was to have him on a chiva—those typical colorful buses from the Colombian towns. But the video was done in two days: one in Medellín and the other in Miami, where the artists were. It was impossible for us to find that chiva in Miami. So, we found a school bus painted with the Colombian flag, we transformed it, and we put José on the roof of the bus.

Willy William

I never told this one to anyone, but do you remember the scene where I'm sitting in a big chair surrounded by girls? I was tired because I really didn't sleep and I was also practicing my lyrics in Spanish and I wasn't feeling comfortable with these parts. I was sitting on this chair and the phone was on my crotch so I could keep my eyes on the lyrics on the phone. I'm acting like I know the words, but I didn't. You don't see that on the video because the whole thing is moving around me. And that's why I'm wearing sunglasses. I was trying to read.

Harold Jiménez

It was a rough video to do. We went to Miami to shoot. The label had advanced us 50 percent of the production costs, but the money had been deposited in our Colombian account, not in the United States. Meantime, I hired a local producer in Miami to set everything up, help us find locations, extras. And two days before the shoot, he said, "You either pay me or I cancel the production." I told him, "Brother, it takes more than twenty-four hours to transfer the money to the United States from Colombia. I give you my word you'll get your money." He said, "No. If the money's not here by tomorrow at noon, I'm canceling." You can't imagine the stress. I was twenty-six years old. I couldn't begin to imagine calling the label, calling José to tell them the video was off. Willy William had come in from France. We had flown in. So, I started calling all my friends to see who could lend me the cash. Literally twelve hours before the shoot, an editor who worked with us saw me so, so overwhelmed that he said, "Dude, let me call my dad and ask if he has a line of credit on his credit cards."

And this dad, this incredibly nice guy, didn't have the cash, but he called his credit cards and asked for an advance. He lent me the money. I was eating at a restaurant in Wynwood, arguing with the producer on the phone, when the call came in. This guy said, "You've helped my son, and I trust you." And he gave me the money.

Fabio Acosta

That song made history by becoming the first all-Spanish-language song to hit #1 on Spotify's global chart. I see it as the song that opened the doors of the world to music in Spanish. It was the song that broke in all the clubs. DJs adopted it. The first time we saw an important DJ play the song, it was at Ultra in Europe. From there, Cedric Gervais, a DJ who lives in Miami, did a remix and the record started to gather steam around the world in the electronic scene, which was a place where music in Spanish had never been that big. "Mi gente" was able to get to places where Latin music had never played on the radio in a big way: Italy, England, Asia. Beyond its being the first Spanish-language song to be #1 globally in streaming, it was the song that really opened the doors for what's happening today with Spanish-language music around the world.

Rebeca León

We really wanted the song to have a general market remix, but we wanted it to live for a while and get as big as it could on a global scale in Spanish. And in that process, we got approached by a lot of people. But when we got word that Beyoncé would be willing to consider doing the track, well, we're big fans of

Beyoncé and we heard that her daughter was obsessed with the song.

Beyoncé's team reached out to Balvin's team, and said, "Blue [Beyoncé and Jay-Z's daughter] really likes this song." At that point Beyoncé wasn't talking about a remix. So we said, "Well, if you're up to it, we would love for you to jump on the song."

J Balvin

Beyoncé's right hand, a great friend of mine, called me and said the queen wanted to get on the remix. I said, "You don't even need to ask."

Jean Rodríguez

I had worked as a vocal coach for Balvin in the past in "Hey Ma." Rebeca hit me up about this Beyoncé thing, except she couldn't tell me it was Beyoncé. It was, "Hey, I need you to come to New York tomorrow. Trust me: It's for a huge artist." She told me it was for "Mi gente" and it was already a monster song, so I knew it had to be huge.

I landed that evening and went to the hotel. I had been in communication with someone who works with Beyoncé, but I didn't know who they were or who they worked for. The next morning, I went down to breakfast and met her in the elevator. And over breakfast I said, "Listen, I gotta ask who I'm working with." And she says, "You're working with Beyoncé." I was speechless for a few seconds, and then just excited. It was a combination of excitement with some nerves. You're gonna work with the baddest vocalist there is. We went to the Hamptons to a temporary studio they had built just so we could get this done. She had her engineer with her and that was it.

Rebeca León

So we sent her the parts. Everything flowed. Truth is, it was all because of Blue. Sky [the track's producer] did her Spanish lyrics. We weren't there when she recorded. Only Jean Rodríguez went there to help her.

Jean Rodríguez

Beyoncé had recorded in Spanish before, but she had never done anything this urban. She was a little worried because the cadence and the rhythmic aspect is different than if you're doing a ballad. When you're doing a bunch of words in Spanish in a line, it takes a little more effort in terms of articulation. We went right at it. She's a sweetheart. She has that southern charm, which is great because it calmed my nerves. When I walked in, she had finished cutting the English part of it. We talked a little bit, she had the lyrics printed, and we started off going line by line. She would repeat after me, and I had her write down on a paper how *she* heard it, which helped out. Every artist is a little different. With her, I recorded her part right there. I laid her part down, and when she got in the booth she was recording on top of my voice until she got comfortable enough that she was able to take my vocal out. You can only push somebody so much in the recording booth. When you tell someone to do it over and over and over a million times, they can get locked out. But she did an amazing job. Obviously, I didn't have to worry about tuning or timing; every take was perfect on that angle. We just really focused on articulation and making sure it sounded authentic. And we also added a little slang. So not only did she have to sing in Spanish properly, but there were some things she had to unproperly say so it fit the song.

When you record in Spanish, words that require rolling the *r*'s can be challenging at times. The endings are very important. There are a lot of words in Spanish that you have to end dry. The *o*'s. It's normal for Americans to open the *oh* instead of closing it. You have to make sure a word like *cantando* sounds like *kan-tan-do* instead of *candandoh*.

It's those little details that go a long way. She was done relatively quickly. She got everything done in three to five hours.

J Balvin

The beautiful thing about "Mi gente" is that it became #1 globally without a remix. And then when Beyoncé jumped into the remix, it became more special. It wasn't a strategy. It just happened. And the fact that all the money she made went to Puerto Rico is a beautiful thing. Because of "Mi gente," Beyoncé invited me to sing with her in Coachella, and after that, I performed alone in Coachella [in 2019] and I headlined Lollapalooza. One was the beginning, the other was the confirmation. Coachella was the beginning of making a statement live. And Lollapalooza proved that it wasn't luck.

Jesús López

From that point on, things changed for José. This reaffirmed his power of persuasion with people. This is a guy who, ever since

I met him, says, "We are going to write a story that will make me a living legend."

Anthony Belolo

Scorpio was already successful. But it would be a lie to say it didn't change the perception of how other people see us. That a global hit can be produced by a local French guy. Maybe we give hope to other young producers in France and Europe and when you have a good song, go for it.

J Balvin

It was key that the song be all in Spanish. I knew the time was right. "Despacito" came before "Mi gente," so the road was already being paved for our Latin movement. I always said the world was ready for another hit, back to back. Before, you had a major Spanish hit every five years. This was immediate. When "Mi gente" started to taper down, we had "X" [with Nicky Jam] and then "I Like It" [with Cardi B and Bad Bunny]. And I think it's only the beginning. That's the dream. To blur that fine line between Spanish and English. I'm a dreamer. Like a good Colombiano, I hustled. I'm super blessed. Let's make more history. This is just the beginning.

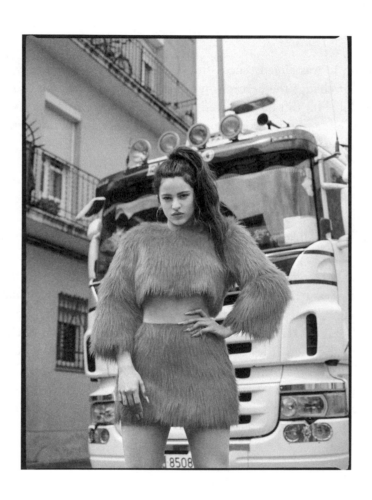

"Malamente"

Rosalía
2018

PLAYERS

Afo Verde: Chairman/CEO of Sony Music Latin-Iberia

C. Tangana (Antón Álvarez Alfaro): Songwriter

El Guincho (Pablo Díaz-Reixa): Producer, songwriter

Rebeca León: Rosalía's manager

Rosalía: Singer, songwriter, producer

In 2018, not only did reggaetón completely dominate Latin music, it was an enormous presence in the global music panorama overall.

Latin music, understood as music predominantly in Spanish, effectively was part of the mainstream, a fixture on the charts and a dominant force on YouTube, where videos by Latin music stars were regularly among the most viewed in the world.

And, for the first time in years, Latin women were having a noticeable impact on the charts.

It was a long time coming. For years, women had been conspicuously absent from the musical spotlight, seemingly relegated to an invisible corner by an onslaught of reggaetón and urban music that they weren't part of. In 2015, only one female artist—Shakira (with Maná)—made it to the top fifty of *Billboard*'s year-end Hot Latin Songs chart. In 2016, there were none. The market was healthy, there was a plethora of male stars, but where were the girls?

"There were always obstacles when you went to radio," says Mayna Nevarez, founder and owner of Nevarez Communications, a PR and marketing firm whose clients include Daddy Yankee and Natti Natasha. "There was an ongoing rhetoric: that women couldn't be too sexy, that they didn't sell, that they were divas and complicated."

It became a self-fulfilling prophecy for years. Until labels, and the industry overall, made a concerted effort to open its eyes and ears to female voices.

The new women also had a new ally in streaming, which allowed them to reach fans directly without interlocutors. The results were highly visible. In 2017, there were eleven tracks led by or featuring female voices among *Billboard*'s Top 50 tracks on the Hot Latin Songs chart. Five of those were Shakira's.

In 2018, the number surged to seventeen, with twelve of those tracks led or co-led by female acts, including newcomers Natti Natasha and Karol G (three each) and Becky G and Anitta (two each).

Outside the United States, in Spain, a different sound was brewing altogether.

A then twenty-five-year-old flamenco singer named Rosalía was making waves in alternative circles with her more contemporary take on venerable traditional Spanish music. Rosalía,

who hailed from Barcelona but had rigorously trained in the
art of flamenco, had released *Los ángeles*, an acclaimed album
among more niche circles, and had drawn the attention of stars
like Alejandro Sanz, who invited her to perform at the Latin
Grammy Person of the Year private gala in the fall of 2017.

There, for the first time, the industry at large got a glimpse
of a prodigious performer with a prodigious voice.

By then Rosalía, an independent artist, was already in conversations with Sony Music in Spain to sign as an artist as she
prepared for her next album, which she would call *El mal querer*
(Bad love). Based on a thirteenth-century novel called *Flamenca*,
it plays like a serial, each song a chapter in a story of ill-fated
love.

What no one knew was exactly what *El mal querer* entailed.
Instead of going the straight-ahead flamenco route, Rosalía
was working with C. Tangana, a well-known Spanish rapper
(and former romantic interest), and with producer Pablo Díaz-
Reixa, known as El Guincho—an electronic producer and artist
known for his sampling, programming, and vocal production.

The first single they put out, "Malamente," was completely
different from anything else happening in Latin music or, for
that matter, in popular music overall. Released in tandem with
a stunning, provocative video full of imagery and Spanish sym-
bolism, "Malamente" broke ranks, visually and musically, amal-
gamating Rosalía's flamenco vocals with loops, beats, and raps,
turning every preconception about her country's iconic musical
tradition on its head. Here was a trained dancer who traded
heels and long-tailed dresses for platform sneakers, midriff-
baring tops, and sweats; a traditional cantaora (flamenco singer)
who collaborated with rappers and reggaetoneros; a thrilling
live performer who mixed hip-hop and flamenco moves with
military precision in front of psychedelic visuals.

A few months later, when Rosalía performed at a Sony convention, "Everyone went crazy. It was as if the Beatles had performed," recalls Sony Latin Chairman Afo Verde.

Despite having no radio airplay and being decidedly outside the realm of "commercial" music, "Malamente" became commercial, and Rosalía became both a lightning rod for criticism from purists and an artistic darling, celebrated by a slew of celebrities hailing from different disciplines, from Billie Eilish and Pedro Almodóvar, to Kylie Jenner and Drake.

Rosalía would indeed go on to sign with Sony. She would win two Latin Grammys for "Malamente," and the following year win four Latin Grammys, including Album of the Year for *El mal querer*. She would become the first artist singing entirely in Spanish to be nominated for Best New Artist at the Grammys. And she would also be the first flamenco act to perform at the Grammys.

"She is exactly the female artist we didn't know we needed," says manager Rebeca León.

"Latin" music—seen in this context as music in Spanish—had finally, truly become global.

Rosalía

"Malamente" was one of the last songs I wrote for the album *El mal querer*. We didn't write it in Barcelona but in Isla El Hierro in the Canary Islands. It's an island where Björk and other artists have gone for inspiration. In El Hierro, we stayed at a house that was almost like a stone cave. It didn't have much light. We went there because we were excited about writing somewhere else. The rest of the album is done in Barcelona, except for "Pienso en tu mirá [I think of your gaze]" and "Malamente." I felt like leaving the house where we had worked on the album for a year,

year and a half. It was necessary to leave and look for different surroundings that would allow us to think differently in order to get different inspiration.

C. Tangana

It seemed like the first single was going to be "A ningún hombre [To no man]," but in the end that wasn't the case. El Guincho, who's from the Canary Islands, suggested we spend a few days on Isla El Hierro, which is a very small island in the Canary Islands, and write and see what came out of that. They had a few beats, but really hadn't done anything. They wanted to be alone to create. And, really, the studio we were at was pretty marginal. It was a house. We went in there and wrote like crazy.

Rosalía

I took my computer and my keyboard. Pablo took his computer. A sound card. A microphone. We took four instruments. Nothing. There was very little [to record with]. I wanted the opening song in the album to be like when a movie begins with a flashback. You watch the opening and you know what's going to happen, you know what the rest of the movie will be. But you still want to watch it. That's the feeling I wanted. I wanted it to explain what the album was about, what was going to happen, provide a brief summary. Just give you the broad strokes of the album and the story. I began to write the lyrics almost a year before we finished it on El Hierro. I started writing alone, and then Antón [C. Tangana] also helped with the lyrics, putting the finishing touches and structure.

C. Tangana

Rosalía wanted to follow a series of chapters in the album, which are based on a novel titled *Flamenca*. The very first chapter had an omen: Something bad was going to happen. [Rosalía had already written a few cuartetas] and I started to write other cuartetas [four-line verses] that had to do with that. Rosalía had given me the subject matter, and I was trying to create coplas [flamenco verses] that could capture what she wanted to say because the concepts were very abstract. They were complicated. We had written several songs by then and it felt like there wasn't a single. We didn't know if this was going to be an introduction or a song. We started to look for a hook. I had the cuartetas but not the melodies, because Rosalía was the melody-maker. I only had the words and we were looking for the hook, and "Malamente" came out of that.

Rosalía

"Malamente" is inspired by the traditional eight-syllable cuarteta flamenca. It's in 4/4, which is a typical flamenco rhythm, but it also has sampling. If you analyze the lyrics, they're inspired by that traditional structure. And the palmas [the handclapping] are on a loop. It's not that someone is playing palmas the whole time. There are three to four seconds of palmas that repeat. It's what we call palmas por tangos flamencos. But the hook is very special. Pablo built it from vocal improvisations I did. I started to improvise words, improvise ad-libs, thinking a little about the feeling of the song. He took those ad-libs, he edited them, and he created that hook, but it all came from vocal improvisation. The verse instead is a melody I wrote inspired by copla flamenca. But it's just the vibe, because in the end it's not traditional at all. It feels catchy. "Malamente" has a catchy verse.

El Guincho

The main core of the song was made really quick. It started as a handclap improv we recorded with Rose. We selected a part that felt great, almost hooky by itself already, then layered that drum pattern on top of it, which ended up being the one you hear in the chorus. We came up with the chord sequence in the afternoon. It was feeling a bit like danzón chords to me, so we added that G on the third chord and that F on the fourth to turn it a little more Phrygian. I layered the 808 [a drum machine] to go with the chords and pretty much had the two sections for the song. I remember I was about to leave the studio, then Rose showed up and I played her the beat. She made that really unique look she does when she's about to do something special. She started improvising some melodies in a voice note, and that ended up being those you hear in the verses, She came up with it really fast.

Rosalía

The part that says "Malamente, si, si. Tra tra," is very repetitive. Those ad-libs are often present in flamenco, as they are in hip-hop. In flamenco we have the jaleos, which are the equivalent of ad-libs in hip-hop. Jaleos are what people say to each other as they play and sing together. For example, if La Perla is singing, the person next to her will say, "Vámonos" or "Vamos allá [C'mon, let's go]." It's very common. So in the end, it's a bit inspired by that.

C. Tangana

Guincho said he wanted to do something like a drop. He wanted those choruses where you only say a word and the beat plays so it becomes a moment to dance. When it says "Malamente" and you hear the ad-libs, that's the "drop," although it wasn't a drop, not really. It's much more sophisticated. Then when the verses come in, the beat is much lower.

El Guincho

I had this idea to make a song for the album with a hook made entirely of ad-libs. The nature of the beat made me think it was the right fit to try it. When I proposed the idea, Rose immediately went with it. We started recording a "library" of jaleos, and right after that I sequenced them on top of the hook drums in a way that felt good, like another rhythmic layer to the drums. Going with that idea for the hook is to me one of the main things that makes Rosalía stand out as an artist, be at a different level, and differentiate herself from her peers. As crazy, challenging, or unusual as anything can be, she will go with it because she knows her talent, level of performance, and persona will make something unique and relevant out of it.

C. Tangana

The sound they were going for was very complicated, because they were looking to add a very sophisticated level of production. We thought it could really become something global, even if it came only from flamenco. Overall, everything they were doing sounded different.

El Guincho

We worked some more on the production. That second verse break came later, as does the whole final sound design for the song. But the main core, both sonically and lyrically, really was made in a day.

To me it's not trap music at all. It's copla. A more modern take on it that draws from other genres, but it still is what it is.

C. Tangana

We started to add the ad-libs. I gave it a pass, then Guincho did another one and changed some of the ones I'd done. Rosalía did another one. And they started to choose which ones would stay and to rerecord them. Suddenly, the ad-libs became very important. In fact, at one point, before they finished the master, they talked about someone else recording them, because they were more urban than flamenco. Very rap. So they wanted someone else to do them to maintain [the flamenco vibe]. But in the end she did them, and those ad-libs—tra-tra-tra—are some of the catchiest things in the record. It's the signature. Yes, it's a bit like looking for the "stupid" element, because it means it's easy to understand. It also implies it's fun. We were looking for flamenco things to say, and words like that—*tra-tra, agua, olé*—are things that are said a lot in flamenco.

Rosalía

Everything we recorded there, stayed there. The "Malamente" takes are from El Hierro. We later rerecorded it in Barcelona, but it had no vibe. So we went back to the first takes and left everything as it was. The palmas, the keyboard Pablo played, the vocal improvisations. Everything is very improvised, raw, and that's how it stayed. I think that's why it sounds like it sounds.

C. Tangana

At one point, I said, "If you don't want this song, I'll record it tomorrow and do the video." In the end, it became the single. Overall, everything we did in El Hierro didn't sound like anything that had been done before. The production was so sophisticated, the R&B sounds they wanted to put in and the flamenco harmonies were a very, very different fusion. I felt it had never been done. Even the words. All the lyrics in the album are inspired by the romancero [Spanish folk ballads] and by that kind of old Spanish manner of speaking. It hadn't been done.

Rosalía

The entire backbone of the album *El mal querer* is conceived at a conceptual level and the song is the opening of that story. And the video—since I didn't know if I was going to make more videos because at the time I wasn't signed as an artist—I wanted it to reflect that universe of inspiration.

The microcosm of *El mal querer* is those flamenco inspirations from the cultural imagination of where I grew up in Barcelona, but also inspired by the south of Spain. I revisited the tradition of bullfighting, for example, but taking it out of context. Instead of an animal, we see a woman on a motorcycle. In the end, I embody the bull. I get into his skin. And that image is a metaphor for this toxic love story that unfolds in the entire album. There are a lot of symbols in the video that are used to explain the story. I think what the director—Nicolás Méndez of [the video production company] Canada—did is brilliant. I simply asked him to re-explain the story and I asked him to use a few of those elements and he created this marvelous video that, madre mía, couldn't be better.

When we left the island, on the plane back to Barcelona, I had what we had recorded on repeat, repeat, repeat, and I had goose bumps. Normally, I don't like to listen to my music. That's not usual. And I thought it was a sign that I believed in the song and that the song was special to me and that it could be special to others.

Rebeca León

She came from making an "alternative" album [*Los ángeles*], not a "commercial" album. She had these songs and she was very convinced about these songs, even though they didn't sound like anything that was out there. I remember that we were in my car at the light between Fifth and Washington in Miami, and she put it on and said, "It's going to be a hit." She was so sure.

Rosalía

Yes, I believed in the song. I was in her car and I had the computer on my lap. I was playing "Malamente" and "Piensa en tu mira." I kept saying, " 'Malamente' is a hit, it's a hit." It's experimental, but it's a hit. I believe in it. It's special. Even though it isn't super accessible, it is. It has that duality. I felt it in my heart. But you do have doubts. I'm not an A&R. I can't listen to something and say, "That's it." I only knew it was big for me.

Rebeca León

We were already in conversations with Sony. But the priority was releasing something in time for the Latin Grammys. You-Tube saw it. So we said, "You know what? Let's put it out on our own, with YouTube's support, and see what happens." "Malamente" exploded. It was much bigger than anyone thought, at an international level.

Afo Verde

I met Rosalía at the Latin Grammys in November. [José María] Barbat [Sony's president in Spain] had spoken to me about her and I met her in person at the Person of the Year gala in 2017. I thought she was from another planet. [A few months later] Rebeca sent me the song. She says, "Tell me what you think." I went crazy. I thought it was absolutely genius, genius, genius. I was most impressed with that combination that I think is genius, which is knowing how to surround yourself well. Rosalía and her team were amazing. They weren't disrespectful to pure flamenco. On the contrary. They went the other direction. They were so respectful that they filled it with modernism. She's an audiovisual artist. She doesn't just think of the audio. You listen to "Malamente," and you hear a song. You see the video and you understand it even more. That's Rosalía. One thing complements the other.

Rebeca León

They supported her a lot on YouTube and it worked. It sparked interest from many artists. The artistic community started to look for Rosalía. The music was incredible, the video was incredible, she was incredible. People always say, "Who is the video director?" I say, "This is Rosalía's vision." She doesn't leave anything to chance.

Afo Verde

I put together a meeting of my managing directors throughout the world specifically for this song. I showed them the track and the video and I said, "If this company can't properly tell the Rosalía story, I don't know what we're here for." It wasn't world music, it wasn't urban, it was Rosalía. A key moment was Lollapalooza en Argentina. Everybody was shouting along to "Malamente." To see that happen, in Buenos Aires, it meant we had done something right. Internally, I reminded the team of Adele and her project. When we started working her into the Latin market, Adele was what the market did *not* need. Our Adele was Rosalía. She went against an entire marketplace. Working a project like that was a little like evangelizing. And nothing would have happened without "Malamente."

C. Tangana

I think it's a banger. It's something very valuable to urban culture and Spanish culture. It's helped people think different, look for a different sound. It's like suddenly originality came into the Latin world. Before, everyone was only thinking about numbers. There was nothing sophisticated, complicated, or risky. There were the Latin rhythms, that Latin flavor that's very characteristic, but there didn't seem to be another option for music in Spanish. That has changed since "Malamente." You can also experiment from the mainstream. That didn't exist before in music in Spanish.

Rosalía

I knew the song could be big, I knew it could be strong. I thought it was the strongest, most accessible track on the album. But I never imagined the impact.

Acknowledgments

Bruno del Granado for insisting this dream was viable; Cristóbal Pera, the Rolls-Royce of editors—how did I get so lucky?; Caitlin Landuyt, whose keen eye and unflagging enthusiasm ushered this manuscript to the finish line; Arthur, who's allowed me to witness firsthand the process of creating and producing music; Allegra and Arturito for your eternal support, love, and back rubs; *Billboard* for your unconditional support; José Feliciano, Los Tigres del Norte, Julio Iglesias, Gloria and Emilio Estefan, Willie Colón, Juan Luis Guerra, Los Del Río, Carlos Vives, Selena, Elvis Crespo, Carlos Santana, Ricky Martin, Shakira, Daddy Yankee, Marc Anthony, Enrique Iglesias, Luis Fonsi, J Balvin, and Rosalía for letting me tell the stories behind your songs.

And to the extraordinary roster of executives, producers, songwriters, and musicians who gave me their time and memories to help tell the world what really happened: Rick Jarrard, Susan Feliciano, Albert Hammond, Enrique "Kiki" García, Jeffrey Shane, Sergio Rozenblat, Omar Alfanno, Marty

Sheller, Roger Zayas, Amarilys Germán, Alvaro de Torres, Jesús López, Jammin Johnny Caride, Carlos de Yarza, Iván Benavides, Mayté Montero, Egidio Cuadrado, Abraham Quintanilla, José Behar, Roberto Cora, Oscar Llord, Rob Thomas, Itaal Shur, Clive Davis, Desmond Child, Draco Rosa, Randy Cantor, Tommy Mottola, Jerry Blair, Angelo Medina, Tim Mitchell, Francisco Saldaña, Carlos Pérez, Gustavo López, Afo Verde, Julio Reyes, RedOne, Descemer Bueno, Gente de Zona, Erika Ender, Mauricio Rengifo, Andrés Torres, Scooter Braun, Juan Felipe Samper, Monte Lipman, Fabio Acosta, Anthony Belolo, Harold Jimenéz, Rebeca León, Jean Rodríguez, Willy William, El Guincho, C. Tangana.

Photo Credits